Praise for *Unstuffed*

As women, we have the tendency to overstuff our lives, our schedules, and our homes with things that really aren't beneficial. And our souls suffer because of our unwillingness to let go. Ruth Soukup tackles this issue head-on and gives practical steps to be purposeful with the stuff we let into our sacred spaces. You'll be thankful you chose this book!

Lysa TerKeurst, *New York Times* bestselling author
and president of Proverbs 31 Ministries

We live in a world that constantly tells us we need to do more, have more, and be more. It's exhausting, and consistently the only thing we ever have more of is stress. Ruth Soukup is like a breath of fresh air as she calls us to declutter our lives and embrace simplicity. If you find yourself tired, stressed, or overwhelmed, then let the words in this book wash over you, and take a deep breath. It's the literary equivalent of a bubble bath and a hot cup of coffee on a cold morning.

Melanie Shankle, *New York Times* bestselling
author of *Nobody's Cuter Than You*

Through powerful story and practical application, Ruth Soukup will help you unstuff your home. But more than that, her words will inspire you to live your most fulfilling life by discarding anything that distracts you from it.

Joshua Becker, founder of *BecomingMinimalist.com* and
Wall Street Journal bestselling author of *Simplify*

This book is excellent. In a culture where women are overwhelmed with things and to-do lists, Ruth Soukup helps us slow down and take inventory of all that is cluttering our lives. *Unstuffed* gives women the tools they need to declutter their homes, minds, and souls through Ruth's transparent stories, struggles, and solutions. I recommend this book not only to moms but to dads too!

Courtney Joseph, founder of *WomenLivingWell.org* —
home of Good Morning Girls

Extremely practical and highly engaging, *Unstuffed* teaches us how to live a life of less. Not just less "stuff" around us, but also less cluttering of our minds and souls. I desperately needed this book! Ruth Soukup does it again.

Ruth Schwenk, founder of *thebettermom.com* and
coauthor of *Hoodwinked: Ten Myths Moms Believe
and Why We All Need to Knock It Off*

It's hard to admit you need *Unstuffed*, but you'll breathe a sigh a relief when you're done. Ruth unpacks why clutter is so detrimental to our minds, homes, and souls. Then she provides easy ways to tackle it. I'm ready to unstuff for the long haul.

Courtney DeFeo, author of *In This House, We Will
Giggle* and founder of Lil Light O' Mine

Unstuffed is proof of why Ruth Soukup is one of America's favorite writers. Practical, transparent, and chock full of tips and biblical wisdom, *Unstuffed* lays out a clear road map from consumerism to contentment. A must-read for women longing to declutter their homes, minds, and souls.

Emily T. Wierenga, founder of The Lulu Tree and author of
Atlas Girl and *Making It Home* (*www.emilywierenga.com*)

More clothes than we need, more emails than we can read, paper mess, kid-toys chaos, dishes overflowing the sink, and shelves jammed with décor, memorabilia, and more — without noticing my life became stuffed and, as a result, my soul cluttered. If you're anything like me, *Unstuffed* grants the reprieve you're longing for. Take a deep breath as Ruth Soukup guides you through the process of decluttering your home, mind, and soul, sharing how she conquered her struggle with organization. Jam-packed with practical strategies, *Unstuffed* doesn't provide a one-time clean-out plan but guides you into solid lifelong principles and systems, kicking the mess to the curb forever. With an encouraging and empowering voice, Ruth challenges us to cast our eyes on the things in life that really count. We don't have to live overwhelmed anymore! This book provides the clear path to an ordered and meaningful life.

Cherie Lowe, author of *Slaying the Debt Dragon: How One Family Conquered Their Money Monster and Found an Inspired Happily Ever After*

Unstuffed graciously reveals why our homes and hearts fill up with junk and gracefully unveils the beauty of letting it go. If you're ready for a clear method to end chaotic messes, Ruth Soukup points the way to simple yet passionate living.

Rachel Wojo, blogger and author of *One More Step*

Do you ever vow to get your act together — finally getting things organized — but then don't know just how and where to start? *Unstuffed* will help you declutter your home, free up much-needed brain space, and spiritually settle your soul.

Karen Ehman, *New York Times* bestselling author of *Keep It Shut* and speaker for Proverbs 31 Ministries unstuffed

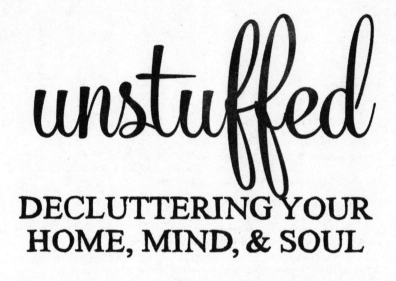

unstuffed

DECLUTTERING YOUR HOME, MIND, & SOUL

RUTH SOUKUP

ZONDERVAN

Unstuffed
Copyright © 2016 by Ruth Soukup

Requests for information should be addressed to:
Zondervan, 3900 Sparks Dr. SE, Grand Rapids, Michigan 49546

Library of Congress Cataloging-in-Publication Data

Names: Soukup, Ruth, 1978-
Title: Unstuffed : decluttering your home, mind, & soul / Ruth Soukup.
Description: Grand Rapids : Zondervan, 2016.
Identifiers: LCCN 2015031891| ISBN 9780310337690 (softcover) | ISBN
    9780310337744 (ebook)
Subjects: LCSH: Simplicity—Religious aspects—Christianity.
Classification: LCC BV4647.S48 S63 2016 | DDC 646.7—dc23 LC record available at
    http://lccn.loc.gov/2015031891

Published in association with The Fedd Agency, P.O. Box 341973, Austin, TX 78734.

Cover design: Curt Diepenhorst
Cover illustration: © koosen / Shutterstock® / © -Oxford- / iStockphoto®
Interior design: Kait Lamphere

First Printing February 2016 / Printed in the United States of America

For Linda and Marie —
you are loved, missed, and always in our hearts

Contents

Part One: HOME

Part Two: MIND

Part Three: SOUL

PART ONE

Home

one

Living

Creating a Vision
for Your Home

*Hospitality is not inviting people to our perfect
homes; it is inviting them to our imperfect hearts.*

Edie Wadsworth

I have a love-hate relationship with stuff.

I love to get stuff.

I love to give stuff.

I love the idea of stuff.

I love getting a good deal on stuff.

Stuff is pretty. Stuff makes me happy.

Stuff makes my home feel cozy.

Except when it doesn't.

Because, then, I hate stuff.

I hate living with stuff.

I hate the way too much stuff makes me feel.

I hate having to clean stuff.

I hate shuffling stuff around.

Stuff is messy. Stuff makes me discontent.

Stuff makes my home feel cluttered.

And the battle rages on.

In my home, this battle of stuff is one that has been going on for years, as long as my husband and I have been together. I'd like to think it is not entirely our fault. We are merely victims of our circumstances.

You see, in 2004, when Chuck and I met, we each had a home of our own, each filled with our own stuff. We merged those two homes into one, but the stuff didn't really coordinate all that well, so we bought new stuff, trying to somehow merge our two different styles into one. What we couldn't make work, we stuffed in the garage.

And then, on August 13, Hurricane Charley struck our home in Punta Gorda, Florida, and suddenly we had a whole new fiasco on our hands. Our little three-bedroom bungalow was badly damaged and in need of major repair—new windows, new doors, new floors, a new roof. We saved money by acting as our own general contractor and doing much of the work ourselves, but in addition to all the stuff we already had, we now had to deal with construction stuff, home repair stuff, and make-it-pretty-again stuff. And our garage filled with even more stuff.

In 2006, we decided to move to Washington State and leave all that Florida stuff behind, at least for a while. We cleared out one bedroom by shoving all that stuff into the other bedroom, and we let a renter move in with all of *her* stuff.

Three years and two kids later, we moved back to Florida with a truckload of—you guessed it—more stuff we had picked up along the way. Our tenant moved out but left a lot of her stuff behind. Naturally, we determined that the solution to our growing stuff problem was to remodel nearly every room in the house and finally complete our hurricane repairs, in the process accumulating *even more* stuff. By this time, our garage was now so full of stuff that we had given up all hope of ever actually parking a car in there again.

And then, in 2011, my mother-in-law died, and we inherited a *whole house* full of eighty-five years' worth of stuff. While we didn't keep *all* of it, we kept enough that a storage unit was the only solution for our growing pile of stuff. When my sister-in-law died in 2013 and we, her closest living relatives, inherited *another whole house* full of stuff, our storage unit was already full.

■ QUICK WINS ▬▬▬▬▬▬▬▬▬▬▬▬

FIVE EASY DECLUTTERING PROJECTS THAT WILL TRANSFORM YOUR LIVING SPACE

While unstuffing your living space might seem like a daunting (or downright impossible) task, many quick and relatively painless decluttering projects can be tackled in small bites that don't take too much time. These small wins can help build confidence without being too overwhelming, and just one or two small projects a week can add up to a big change over time.

PROJECT 1
Create a Collection Zone

Designate one area, whether it's the corner of your living room or laundry room, the entry hall, the stairway, or any other space that makes sense for your home and family, to capture all the stray items that need to be put away each day—shoes, books, toys, etc.

Use a pretty box, bin, or basket to collect all the items throughout the day and then schedule a time each day to empty the basket and put things away. A great way to remember to do this, at least until it becomes a habit, is to set an alert on your phone to go off at the same time each day.

For maximum success and lasting results, be sure to get the whole family involved in the process. Reserve ten minutes before bedtime for putting things away, or consider giving each family member their own basket for which they are responsible.

PROJECT 2
Clear the Counters

Chaotic countertops can make your entire living space feel oppressive. Cooking becomes a burden and a chore, and a thorough cleanup feels impossible. But it doesn't have to be. Creating a clutter-free zone in the kitchen will make a huge difference for the overall feel of your home, and committing to keep it that way will transform the way you cook and clean.

Start by tossing out the obvious junk, whether it's random paperwork, old food, broken dishes or appliances, or anything else no longer in use. Next, put away anything taking up counter space that already has a home. Remove everything that is left so that all counters are completely clear, wash them well, and then put back on the counter only the appliances you use more than once a week. Finally, consider selling or donating any items you don't use regularly, or find new homes for items that don't yet have a place.

PROJECT 3
Sweep the Surfaces

Even a clean house can feel cluttered and chaotic when every horizontal surface, every table and bookshelf and mantel and ledge, is covered with *stuff*. This can be true even when the stuff—books, picture frames, candles, figurines, vases, bowls, and everything in between—is intended to be decorative and pretty.

Even if you love your things, consider putting them away for a month or two, just to see how it feels. Do a clean sweep of every item on every surface in your living room. Take down all the items, box them up, and put the boxes aside for at least four to six weeks. Pay attention to how this makes you feel. Do you miss your stuff, or can you breathe easier without it? What items do you miss the most? At the end of your experiment, put back only those items you truly missed, and then sell or donate the rest.

PROJECT 4
Pitch the Pillows

Like surface clutter, throw pillows, blankets, and other soft goods that are meant to be decorative often end up doing little more than adding to the chaos. Consider this: Are your pillows really all that decorative if they are constantly on the floor?

I can totally understand your reluctance to let them go—I was the exact same way. In fact, it wasn't until I lost a bet to my husband in which the wager was him tossing out all our throw pillows that I realized how much cleaner our living room seemed without them. If you can't imagine getting rid of them for good, try taking them away for a month and see how it feels.

PROJECT 5
Manage the Media

Books, magazines, DVDs, and video games can quickly turn into a disorganized mess if not dealt with on a regular basis. If your media library has grown out of control, it is time to reel it back in and pare it down to only those items you will read (or watch or play) again. The rest has to go.

Pick *one* pile—whether it's books or DVDs or magazines or video games—to tackle at a time. Gather all of them into one place and ask yourself, honestly, *Will we ever read (or watch or play) this again?* If the answer is no, get it out of the house. Sell it, donate it, or toss it, but get it out. Repeat the process with your remaining media until you've sorted through all of it.

We were drowning.

We *are* drowning.

And I look around at all this stuff—some of it nice stuff, some of it sentimental stuff, some of it useful stuff, some of it pretty stuff, some of it expensive stuff, some of it inherited stuff, but *almost all of it unnecessary stuff*—and I wonder, honestly:

Will we ever become UNstuffed?

Drowning Together

I'm pretty sure I'm not the only one who feels like stuff has completely taken over their lives. In my home, the catalyst for chaos was an *actual* natural disaster, but ultimately the responsibility for the mess lies in the choices I've made along the way. And so it is for each one of us. We each have our own hurricanes. Some are just a little more metaphorical than others.

Some time ago, I hosted a "31 Days to a Clutter-Free Life Challenge" on my blog, LivingWellSpendingLess.com. Readers were invited to sign up to have daily challenges sent straight to their inbox for an entire month, and each day we would tackle one specific area of our homes. I was doing the challenge more to deal with my own stuff problem than anything else, but I thought it might be fun to have a few people join me for a few weeks of online moral support. How great would it be to have a few dozen friends cheering me on, while I did the same for them?

Imagine my surprise when more than *fifty thousand* readers joined the clutter-free challenge that month! Fifty thousand people wanting to figure out a way to rid their life of clutter. Fifty thousand people with too much stuff. Fifty thousand people wanting to clear out the chaos, once and for all.

In the time since then, thousands more readers have taken that same challenge, which is now available in book form. Many have contacted me personally to share their own struggles with stuff. Some share how years of shopping addictions have filled their homes with piles of stuff they can't seem to get rid of—a struggle I can relate to all too well. Some share how going without stuff as children made them turn to excess as adults. They grew up not being able to afford anything, and overcompensated by wanting *everything*. Some explain that the problem isn't their clutter, but their spouses, who won't let anything go, or their parents, who keep showering them or their children with more and more stuff they don't need or want but feel they can't get rid of because, well, it was a gift. Some can't resist a bargain or a garage sale or a thrift store find. They've filled their home to the brim with deals that were just too good to pass by. Others are trying to fill a hole that seems insatiable. Always convincing themselves that this next thing will be the one that makes them whole. But it never does.

They are all drowning.

In one way or another, I think *all* of us are drowning. We are all drowning in a sea of unrelenting clutter—this *stuff*—that threatens to wash us away unless we somehow learn how to swim.

Sadly, it's not even just the physical stuff that has taken over our homes. We are often overwhelmed by mental and spiritual clutter too. Our schedules fill up; the piles of paperwork build up; and the margin we need just to breathe feels nonexistent. We work so hard, in so many different ways, always wanting and hoping and longing to be enough. Every square inch is filled, but with what? When will enough be enough? Why is there never room for the things that actually matter?

But more importantly, *how do we change the pattern?*

How do we become unstuffed?

I'm just going to warn you right now that this book is *not* a step-by-step guide on how to declutter your home. I won't walk you room by room through the process of physically decluttering your space or provide checklists for each zone. I've already written that challenge.

Oh, don't get me wrong, this book will include many practical tips along the way. Each chapter will offer sidebars of concrete ideas you can implement right away to clear the chaos and create calm, clutter-free zones within your home. But becoming unstuffed is much more than getting rid of the things you no longer want. It's more than getting organized or finally taming that pile of paperwork that's been taunting you.

Becoming unstuffed, *truly* unstuffed, is much more than that.

It's changing the way we look at our homes and the stuff we live with.

It's changing the way we look at our schedules and the stuff that fills our time.

It's changing the way we look at our relationships and the stuff they are made of.

It's becoming purposeful about the stuff we let in, because the reality is that nature hates a vacuum, and if we are to become unstuffed, we better spend some time thinking about what that really means before our unstuffing stuffs us with new stuff we don't need or want. (Say that five times fast!) But as funny as that may sound, the reality is serious business: We have to choose our stuff well, or it may just bury us alive.

In our homes, it means spending some time thinking about what we actually want our homes to be rather than simply what items we no longer want or use. It means thinking about how we use our home, how we want to use it, who we share it with, and ultimately how we want it to make us feel.

I love William Morris's famous quote: "Have nothing in your houses that you do not know to be useful, or believe to be beautiful."[1] These are words to live by, and as we think about what it means to become unstuffed, I hope we will take these words to heart and apply them to our homes in the most practical ways. But I also think change, real change, has to come from a deeper place. It has to come from a place where we examine our motives and where we understand what got us into this predicament in the first place. After all, if we can't stop the flow of new stuff coming in, all the books in the world about organizing and decluttering won't help.

10 TIDY HABITS THAT WILL CHANGE YOUR LIFE

It's easy to think of all the good habits we *wish* we had. And, as it turns out, setting good habits can be a powerful way to achieve our goals, as well as keep us focused and organized. Once a good habit becomes etched in our brain, we're able to attain our objectives without even thinking about it.

In his bestselling book *The Power of Habit*, Charles Duhigg discusses the ways we use habits to achieve the things we want.[2] He explains that habits require three components—the cue, the reward, and the routine. In order to successfully create any automatic response, we have to nail all three.

The *cue* is simply the circumstances surrounding the habit. Take, for example, brushing your teeth, which you (hopefully) do at least twice a day. Most likely you do it when you wake up and before going to bed. You probably brush in the bathroom. You're also probably by yourself, or maybe your spouse is there too. You may be triggered or *cued* to do it because, well, your mouth tastes mucky or you ate something with garlic in it. Most of us don't think much about brushing our teeth; we just do it out of habit. We don't spend hours anticipating the act or even thinking about it at all. It just gets done.

The *reward* is whatever helps trigger that "muscle memory" or Pavlovian response. In classical conditioning, animals (or humans) are given a cue to perform a task and then rewarded with a treat. Eventually, just the presence of the cue will trigger a response. Whether it's a habit in budget keeping, exercise, or even dental hygiene, a reward is a mandatory part of the process. Good habits produce good results. In our teeth-brushing example, the reward is a clean mouth, a lower dental bill, lack of mouth pain, and maybe even the fact that you'd rather avoid a lecture from your dental hygienist.

The *routine* is simply putting the cue, the act, and the reward together. Once you combine these three components—(1) My mouth feels mucky; (2) I brush my teeth; (3) my mouth feels better—you have the recipe for a good habit.

But here's the cool part, and the big reason creating good habits matters so much: *Habits, once established, use a different part of our brain.* We don't have to think about them; we just do them, and they don't drain our mental energy. Thus, the more good habits we can create, the more productive, happier, and successful we can become. When it comes to keeping our homes tidy and free of clutter, taking the time to develop good habits can literally be the difference between chaos and calm. For the next four weeks, why not work on incorporating these ten tidy habits into your daily routine? They might just change everything.

1. **Make your bed** (*time commitment: 2 minutes*). What else can you do in just a minute or two that will completely transform your entire room? It doesn't really matter how messy the rest of the room happens to be; when the bed is made, your bedroom looks tidy. Simplify the task by choosing fuss-free bedding that is easy to straighten and by eliminating decorative pillows or throws.

2. **Clean the kitchen sink** (*time commitment: 10–15 minutes, 3 times a day*). In the same way that a neatly made bed can transform the bedroom, a shiny, sparkling sink can be the difference between cluttered and cozy in the kitchen. Make it a habit to keep your sink clear—putting dishes straight into the dishwasher or hand-washing as you go.

3. **Toss your junk mail** (*time commitment: 1 minute*). Sorting and tossing your junk mail, catalogs, and flyers the instant they come into the house can help keep paper clutter to a minimum and your mail pile under control. While our

temptation is to throw the whole stack on the counter and get to it later, the truth is that tossing as you go takes only a few seconds.

4. **Pick up** (*time commitment: 10 minutes*). This is a daily habit the whole family can participate in! Set an alert on your phone to remind you of "Operation Cleanup" each day, and for ten minutes, everyone in the house works to pick up any items left lying around. Cleanup time can be just before bed, right after school, or even first thing in the morning, as long as it is consistent.

5. **Keep the table clear** (*time commitment: 5 minutes*). A messy, cluttered table not only brings disorder and chaos to an entire room; it disrupts mealtimes and inhibits families from sitting down to eat together. Make your table a clutter-free zone, and, if necessary, spend a few minutes keeping it clean and clear each day.

6. **Clear and wipe down your bathroom counters** (*time commitment: 3 minutes*). Between the toothpaste, toothbrushes, makeup, hair products, and more, our bathrooms can easily become clutter zones without daily vigilance. Make it a daily habit to clear the counter as soon as you're done getting ready for the day, and then take a moment to wipe down any mess you may have left behind.

7. **Do one load of laundry** (*time commitment: 3 minutes to start; 2 minutes to transfer; 5 minutes to fold*). The never-ending pile of laundry can be a challenge for even the most diligent of homemakers. However, making it a daily habit to tackle just one load can help tame that beast and keep the laundry clutter under control. Start your load at the same time every day, and before you know it, you won't even have to think about it.

8. **Put your clothes away** (*time commitment: 3 minutes*). Clean clothes are wonderful, but not if they pile up on the counter or in the laundry basket and never actually make it to the closet or dresser. It only takes a few minutes to put away clothes that have been washed and folded, and it takes even less time to take care of the clothes you're finished wearing for the day. Put them away as you're changing, and your clothing clutter will be a thing of the past.

9. **Bring your inbox to zero** (*time commitment: 10–15 minutes*). Physical clutter isn't the only kind of clutter that can weigh us down on a daily basis. While we'll talk a lot more in chapter 5 about dealing with digital clutter, developing a daily habit of conquering your inbox can greatly impact your sense of calm. Be quick to delete messages, and keep your responses brief and to the point.

10. **Plan your day** (*time commitment: 5 minutes*). Five minutes in the morning to go over your schedule and create your to-do list for the day can spell the difference between actually getting things done and simply spinning your wheels. Make it a habit to pause and plan, and you'll soon find you're able to accomplish far more than ever before.

As we work our way through *this* book, I'd like us to take the approach found in Hebrews 12:1: "Let us throw off everything that hinders and the sin that so easily entangles. And let us run with perseverance the race marked out for us." This means not just throwing out those things we no longer want or need, though that is an important part of the process, but *actively striving for the end goal*. In order to get there, we need to have a clear picture of what that end goal looks like.

What does it mean to be unstuffed?

How Do You Use Your Home?

While my husband is a true extrovert, happily striking up a conversation with anyone anywhere, I tend to be slightly more introverted, often feeling shy and awkward in social situations. Nevertheless, we both love entertaining in our home, whether it be hosting a few close friends for a casual game night or fifty acquaintances for a lively summer bash. Over the years, we have thrown some wonderful — and occasionally over-the-top — parties, but we've also more recently begun to realize we are just as happy hosting an impromptu last-minute gathering with takeout Chinese food and a Lego-strewn floor as we are when we host an elaborate themed affair complete with Pinterest-worthy decorations and menu to match. To us, the important thing is that we take the time to really connect with our friends and family, and we've tried to set up our home accordingly.

While our three-bedroom, two-bathroom home certainly isn't small, it's not particularly big either. This past Thanksgiving, we tested its limits when my brother Paul; his wife, Jackie; and their three grown children, Jacob, Hannah, and Sarah, came to stay for a week, along with Hannah's fiancé, also named Jacob. We knew it was going to be a tight squeeze with all of us, but we were ready. Sarah and Hannah would sleep in my girls' room, which has a bunk bed that can sleep four. My two young daughters, Maggie and Annie, would share the full bed, while Sarah could take the top bunk, and Hannah the trundle. Paul and Jackie would be comfortable in the guest room, and the two Jacobs would sleep in the living room, one on the hide-a-bed, and the other on the sofa. It would be tight, but we'd make it.

And then, a few days before Thanksgiving, we got the news that another niece — my sister's college-age daughter, Coryn, who plays soccer for the South Carolina Gamecocks — would be playing in the Elite Eight game at Florida State after upsetting the higher-ranked North Carolina team in their Sweet Sixteen game. The Elite Eight! This was a pretty big deal, since her team had never made it that far in Coryn's time there. And although Tallahassee is six hours away, it was also a big deal that she would be playing anywhere close to us, especially since the rest of my family lives in Washington State, three thousand miles away. My sister Beth—Coryn's mom—immediately made plans to fly to Florida for Thanksgiving so we could all drive up to FSU the next day to cheer on our favorite soccer star.

But then, just after booking the flight, Beth had second thoughts. "Are you sure it's okay for me to stay with you? Maybe I should find a hotel. You've already got a full house! Won't you be stressed-out with all those people everywhere?"

After assuring her that I wouldn't be stressed, and that the girls would be perfectly fine—perhaps even happier—camping out on the floor in our bedroom, and that, no really, they don't need a bed, and that no really, we'll have enough food, and that no really, we couldn't wait for her to come for Thanksgiving, and that, *no really*, it would all be fine, she *finally* started to relax.

I'm not going to lie—it was a *very* full house that week. There were occasional lines for the bathrooms and a nearly constant stream of dirty coffee cups—we all *really* like our coffee—and although we had cleaned the house from top to bottom beforehand, it looked like a bomb had gone off from the moment everyone arrived.

None of that mattered.

We had *such* a good time—without a doubt some of the best times I've ever had with my family—and made memories I will never, ever forget. Our Thanksgiving dinner, which came together as a team effort, ended with every single one of us shedding tears of genuine joy and gratitude as we shared, honestly and sincerely, our highs and lows from the year. We stayed up until the wee hours of the morning, chatting and laughing and enjoying each other's company. We made homemade signs for the big game, dressed from head to toe in black and crimson, and cheered our hearts out for Coryn as her team was thoroughly crushed 5–0. But even that utter annihilation turned out okay, because, with her season now over, we were allowed to take

Coryn back to Punta Gorda with us. By that point, we just figured the more, the merrier! We took an airboat ride and laughed for hours about my sister's complete freak-out while attempting to hold a baby alligator. We took a billion goofy group selfies and played silly games. We even made the obligatory southern road trip stop at Waffle House. (Who knew you could feed twelve people at a restaurant for just $80?) Then we went home and simply enjoyed each other's company for a few more days.

It was perfect, precisely because it was all so *imperfect*.

When I think about how I use my home, or how I *want* to use my home, *that* is the memory that comes to mind. The reason that time meant so much to me was that, over the past few years, it is precisely the vision I have been striving for. I want my home to be a place where the people I love can gather. I want my home to be a place where my focus is not on whether my flat-screen TV is big enough or my décor stylish enough or my food gourmet enough, but instead on how welcome and wanted and right-at-home everyone feels when they walk through the door.

It hasn't always been that way for me.

I'm not proud to admit there have been plenty of times in the not-too-distant past when I was far more worried about the image than the reality. When my version of hospitality was all about me and the attention I could bring to myself rather than about how I made others feel. I wanted my home to look like it belonged in the Pottery Barn catalog, and I spent a lot of time and energy — not to mention far too much money — trying to make it look that way.

I bought fancy leather furniture for the living room, paid way too much for a faux-industrial, hand-distressed table in the dining room, and fell in love with an overpriced duvet cover for the bedroom. Within months, it was all ruined. Our chocolate Lab, Lita, despite every effort to keep her off, somehow managed to scratch up the couch beyond repair. My youngest daughter, Annie, who was about eighteen months old at the time, took a black Sharpie to the matching leather ottoman and also proceeded to hammer out deep, decidedly *non*artful gouges in our artfully distressed table—and then, with a ball-point pen, added her own designer touches to our duvet cover. There was a reason her nickname used to be "Trouble"!

In hindsight, buying a bunch of expensive brand-new furniture with a stubborn eighty-pound dog and a hell-bent-on-destruction toddler running around was probably a really bad idea, a disaster in the making that anyone from the outside looking in—including my husband—could have spotted a mile away. But I didn't see it. All I saw were those pretty catalogs full of things I wanted, things I thought would make me happy and satisfy the longing I felt deep inside.

What kind of heartache (not to mention money!) could I have saved had I been more honest with myself about the stage of life we were in at that moment? If I had realistically looked at all the dog-eared catalogs and magazine clippings and decided that my home needed to reflect how we *actually* used it, not how *House Beautiful* said it could look?

Because now? Five years later, that beat-up, scratched-up leather couch still serves our purposes just fine. And the coffee table that we never got around to replacing? Well, it might not look quite right and it might be full of dings and scuff marks, but no one ever has to use a coaster, and it also makes a fantastic stage for our aspiring performers. Our artfully distressed table gets just a little more "character" added to it every day. And the duvet cover? Well, it has two sides. Besides, we live in Southwest Florida. No one really needs a comforter here anyway.

It was a tough lesson, but I've learned that the very first step toward becoming unstuffed is being realistic about how we *actually* use our homes rather than how we *think* we should use them. After all, filling our homes with things we don't need based on a fantasy that will never actually materialize is nothing more than an exercise in frustration. Instead, when we're honest with ourselves and with our spouses about the purpose and function of our living space, it becomes easier to sift out the things that matter from the things that only add to the chaos.

How do you use your home? What is its purpose? Is it a place to play? Is it a place to work or earn a living? Is it a place of learning? Is it a place of studying or teaching? Do you homeschool there? Is it your sanctuary, your place to relax and rewind after a long day? Is it a gathering place, or a place where you want to bring people together? Is it a foodie paradise, a place where good food and conversation are of the utmost importance? Is it a place of artwork or crafts, or a place to be inspired? Is it a place of cinema and television, or one where sports are at the center? What is the purpose of your home? More importantly, is its purpose what you want it to be?

Who Do You Share Your Home With?

In my midtwenties, after I had finally begun to recover from a deep depression that consumed several years of my early adulthood, I got a job managing an apartment complex called Brampton Court. The job was a live-in position, which meant that for the first time in my life, I was going to have my very own place. The apartment was badly in need of new carpet and paint, so the very kind maintenance man let me choose the colors rather than just going with the standard-issue white. After nearly three years of darkness and despair, all I wanted were bright, bold, happy colors — lime green for the living room, coral for the bedroom, and pale yellow for the bathroom. My tiny budget afforded only the barest of basics from Ikea, but it was cute and it was fun and it was *mine*.

You see, in college I had lived in the dorms for a year and then shared a duplex with three roommates for a year, until I got married the summer between my sophomore and junior years. It was the two of us for a year, and then for my senior year of college, my two teenage brothers moved in, which made for a very odd dynamic, especially given that our marriage wasn't going particularly well. After that ill-fated marriage finally fell apart, and while I fought my battle with depression, I bounced from hospital to hospital, staying with friends and family in between. So until I got my pretty, little apartment at 1600 Birchwood Avenue, I never had a place entirely my own.

I loved every minute of it.

In my own little apartment, I could stock the fridge with whatever odd foods I wanted. I could watch the shows that interested me, read books for hours on end, and listen to the music I loved. It was easy to keep clean, and everything was always neat, tidy, and very organized. And while I got a dog and started to make new friends and enjoyed going out, it was there that I also learned to enjoy being alone.

I've been married to my second husband, Chuck, for ten years now, and while I wouldn't change a thing, I still look back at that period of living alone as one of the most important times in my life. Those years shaped me and molded me and helped me come into my own as a person, and as an adult. I learned to budget my time and my money, to take responsibility for myself, to cook and clean and get things done. There was no one else there to do it for me. And yes, if I'm being perfectly honest, sometimes, every once in a while, I do miss having my own quiet space.

Our home is very different now, not just in the way it looks, with its muted earth tones and classic traditional furniture, but in who I share it with. Long gone are the days when it was just me and my faithful-but-completely-spastic chocolate Lab. Oh, Lita is still around, at least for the moment, but her days are numbered, and, no longer spastic, she spends most of her time sleeping on her favorite scratched-up couch, though she does usually rally long enough to give visitors a few well-placed licks. But I also have Chuck and our two daughters, Maggie and Annie, to share my space with, not to mention a steady stream of friends, both young and old, coming by, whether for a few hours or a few days. Our home is often full and rarely quiet.

I still love every minute of it. Well, *almost* every minute.

As I get older, I'm realizing that *who* I share my home with makes a big difference when it comes to stuff. You see, when it was just me in that small apartment, able to afford only the barest of essentials, stuff wasn't really a problem. It didn't even factor into the equation. I had what I needed, and very little else. Sometimes I think I miss those days, not because I was alone, but because life was just so simple.

The fact is, more people means more stuff. And since we can't really kick out the rest of our family in our effort to become unstuffed, we have to find a balance between respecting the stuff that others bring in and not overstuffing our home to the point of no return. Thus, the critical next step in becoming unstuffed is to think long and hard about who we share our home with and what their needs are.

Who are the people sharing your space? What are their ages? What are their interests? What are their hobbies? What are their needs? What is their tolerance for clutter? Do they want to keep everything, or are they happy to let things go? Are they sentimental? What are the sources of tension between the members of your household? Do you ever argue about tidying? About responsibilities? About money? About how you spend your time? What is the purpose of your home to the people you live with? Is that purpose in line with what you feel your home should be?

How Do You Want Your Home to Feel?

Have you ever walked into someone else's house and felt immediately at home? Like somehow, even though it wasn't really yours, you just *belonged* there? Whether it was the décor, the cozy couch, the steaming-hot cup of coffee, or just the way you felt when you walked in the door, most of us at one point or another have experienced that "I could totally live here" feeling.

For me, it is my friend Stacy's house, a 1930s Craftsman just bursting with character. I love everything about it — the well-worn hardwood floors, the brick fireplace, the beautiful dark wood trim, and the gorgeous built-ins. I also love her quirky vintage style — the way she turns junk into treasure and somehow just makes it all work. Her food is always to-die-for, simple and hearty, made with farm-fresh ingredients and eggs from her very own chickens. I often joke that Stacy is exactly who I want to be when I grow up.

But I love going to Stacy's house, not just because it's beautiful and interesting and she makes really good food, but because she always seems genuinely delighted to see me and genuinely happy to do what she does. She has found her sweet spot, her special niche, and her ability to embrace her own unique style makes her a joy to be around. I love seeing the happiness she gets from reclaiming someone else's castoff, and I love watching her creative energy at work, even if her unique style is far different from my own.

I don't feel at home at Stacy's house because it is free of clutter and totally unstuffed; on the contrary, she has a ton of stuff — albeit really cool vintage stuff — absolutely everywhere, far more than I could ever comfortably live with in my own space. No, I feel at home at Stacy's house because of the way I *feel* when I am there. Happy. Content. Creative. Welcome. Appreciated.

I don't know about you, but that is *exactly* how I want people to feel when they are in my home. I don't want it to be so sterile that they are afraid to touch anything, but I also don't want it to be so messy or full of clutter that they can't move. In the end, becoming unstuffed ultimately means removing everything that doesn't contribute to the way we want our homes to feel, while keeping everything that does. In theory, it is a very simple concept. Of course, the reality can be much more painful.

Close your eyes and think about the way your home actually looks and feels right now. Imagine yourself walking through the front door after being away for the day. When you look around, what do you see? Is the room neat and tidy, with clear surfaces and a home for everything, or is the counter full of dishes, with haphazard paperwork scattered around? Are your things picked up and put away, or do you see clothes and toys covering the floor? Do your windows sparkle in the sunlight, or are they streaked with dust and fingerprints? Does it smell fresh and clean, or does it smell like the garbage needed to be taken out yesterday? How do you feel when you walk in this space? Are you relaxed and happy to be home, or are you instantly tense because you know how much work needs to be done? Do you feel calm, or chaotic? Do you want to sit and stay awhile, or do you want to just turn around and run away?

Our homes are quite possibly the most open and honest reflection of our state of mind that we will ever find. The more cluttered and chaotic we are inside, the more our homes will reflect that confusion. But the opposite is also true. The more we can tame the physical space around us and create an environment that soothes, welcomes, and comforts, the calmer we will feel inside. Once we are aware of how we use our home and who we share it with, we must also take the time to not only consider how we want our home to feel, but commit, right here and right now, to doing whatever it takes to make it feel that way.

■ **FILL IN THE BLANKS** ▬▬▬▬▬

WHAT IS MY VISION FOR MY HOME?

What Is My Decorating Style?

What do I like? What do I not like? Am I drawn to modern looks, or am I more traditional? What are my favorite magazines or blogs? What colors do I like? What do I not like?

_____

_____

_____

_____

_____

_____

_____

How Do I Want My Home to Feel?

What are the words I want others to use to describe my home? How do I want people to feel when they walk in my door? How do I want to feel when I am at home?

_____

_____

_____

_____

_____

_____

_____

How Do I Use My Home?

What are the primary activities I use my home for? Sleep? Work? Play? Entertaining? What hobbies and interests affect the way I use my space?

_____

_____

_____

_____

_____

_____

_____

Who Lives Here?

Name, age _____

Primary activities at home: _____

_____

_____

One change that would accommodate a need/desire:

_____

Name, age _____

Primary activities at home: _____

_____

_____

One change that would accommodate a need/desire:

_____

Name, age _____

Primary activities at home: _____

_____

_____

One change that would accommodate a need/desire:

_____

Name, age _____

Primary activities at home: _____

_____

_____

One change that would accommodate a need/desire:

_____

Name, age _____

Primary activities at home: _____

_____

_____

One change that would accommodate a need/desire:

_____

two

Storage

More Closet Space Is Not the Solution

*The best way to find out what we really need is to
get rid of what we don't.*

Marie Kondo

I live in Southwest Florida, where the highest elevation is approximately ten feet above sea level and basements are otherwise known
as swimming pools. While there are many things I love about this
tropical climate, what I don't always love are the bugs and heat and
humidity — especially when it comes to storage. You see, between the
lack of basements and attic and garage space (because they're rendered
practically useless by the elements), Florida homes have a serious lack
of storage space.

For years, I spent a lot of time complaining about this fact, and
even more time shuffling things around to make them fit. We installed
floor-to-ceiling shelves in each of the four closets, and I bought every
form of bin, box, crate, and basket I could find to try to make it all
fit and look pretty. I kept telling myself that if I could just get it all
organized, if I could just find the right system, it would all be okay.
I'd somehow be able to overcome this lack of storage space and make
it all work.

But all the while, I kept shopping. I'd make the rounds at Target,
bringing home bag after bull's-eye-dotted white bag full of all the

pretty, well-designed things I just knew I couldn't live without — seasonal candles and the newest beach-themed picture frames, adorable dish towels and stylish throw rugs, cleverly embroidered pillows and decorative vase fillers, monogrammed mugs and child-friendly plates, semiautomatic mops and chic designer brooms, ultracute bins and boxes and baskets and storage containers. Oh, the storage containers. Over and over again, I convinced myself that the right boxes would be the solution to my storage problem.

I literally spent hours each week cleaning and sorting and reorganizing all this stuff, trying to make it fit, moving it from bin to basket to box, trying desperately to get it all neat and and tidy, and always wondering why it never seemed to stay that way. And so? I'd head back to Target for another round — for more bins, more baskets, more cleaning supplies, and more *stuff* to solve the problem.

In all that time, it never occurred to me that the problem was not my lack of closet space or the fact that I didn't have an attic or garage or basement to hold all my stuff. My problem wasn't that I hadn't found the right basket or box or bin. My problem wasn't that there weren't enough shelves in the closet or the best hangers or the perfect hooks. My problem wasn't that I hadn't yet found a home for everything, and my problem wasn't that I hadn't found the best system to organize it all.

And then one day, after warning my two young daughters to clean up their room for what must have been the seven millionth time, after telling them over and over and over again that if they couldn't keep their room picked up, I was going to take it all away, I finally had enough. I gathered all the empty boxes I could find — there were plenty to choose from — and packed up all their toys. Every single last one. All their stuffed animals and Barbies and blocks and trains and Littlest Pet Shops and My Little Ponies and Strawberry Shortcakes. All the dolls and dress-up clothes and play food for their kitchen. Every single thing. In one fell swoop, their room was completely clear.

I expected them to freak out, but instead the opposite happened.

BECOME CLUTTER-FREE

F—Fight to Stop the Flow

At every turn, we are bombarded with an overpowering message of consumption—there is always something else to buy! We need to actually FIGHT—fight with ourselves, fight against advertising, fight against a culture that is telling us to buy more, more, more. There are two ways to do this.

First, we have to *eliminate temptation* and simply avoid the stores whenever possible. This means not going to Target or Walmart or even Goodwill if that is your temptation. It means to stop going to garage sales. This is not really about how much you spend; it is about not needing more stuff.

Second, we need to *buy only what is essential*. Make a list and stick to it or obey a twenty-four-hour policy if you are in the store and see something you like. It means no longer buying on impulse, but instead only going to the store if there is something you really, truly need.

R—Reduce by Ruthlessly Purging

Once you've fully committed to fighting the flow and keeping the influx of new stuff out, it is time to tackle the mess you've already made by ruthlessly purging *everything*.

To do this, you must decide to keep only that which is currently useful. If you haven't used it in the past year to eighteen months, stop holding on to it. If you don't love something or if it doesn't bring joy or value to your home, don't let it stay. Give yourself permission to let go of anything you aren't actually using and give it to someone who might get some use out of it.

E—Establish Strict Limits

Adopting a strict limit policy forces us to change our thinking. It reminds us of the fundamental truth that our consumer-driven society so desperately wants us to forget: We already have enough. To do this, we must be persistent about QUANTITY control. In today's society, more and bigger is seen as better, but this isn't necessarily the case. If your clutter is out of control, start setting actual numerical limits on the number of things you will allow yourself to have. Forty hangers in your closet. Eight pairs of shoes. Three sets of dishes. No more than one of each tool in the garage. And so on and so on. You will have to decide for yourself what is a reasonable number, but once you've determined what is reasonable, be diligent about sticking to it.

E—Emphasize Quality over Quantity

We often buy too much stuff because it is cheap and readily available, when we should take a totally different approach and instead choose long-term value over short-term savings. This doesn't mean spending whatever we want and only buying the most expensive items, but it does mean that sometimes paying a little more for something that will last is a much smarter tactic.

Adopting this philosophy also means committing to buy things that are well made from quality materials. In the end, it is so much better to invest in one quality piece that will stand the test of time than to have to replace a cheap, poorly made item again and again.*

---

*For instructions on how to get a free printable version of this list that you can hang in your home, see page 219 at the back of the book.

They watched in stunned silence for a few minutes and then started to help. But the real surprise for me came in the next few days and weeks.

They were actually *happier*. Instead of complaining that they had nothing to do, they found lots to do. They stopped fighting; started playing better together; began reading, coloring, and writing more; and learned to use their imagination.

That moment was a turning point for our entire family, *but especially for me*. I began to reevaluate everything. I realized for the very first time that the problem wasn't that my house was deficient, or that I didn't have big enough closets, or that I hadn't yet found the right way to organize it all. My problem, pure and simple, was those bull's-eye-dotted white plastic bags. And the paper ones from all my other favorite stores. And the boxes arriving far too frequently from Amazon.com. In fact, my problem wasn't a lack of storage space at all.

My problem was too much stuff.

Fight to Stop the Flow

Some of our most profound lessons in life come through our children, and in my case, it was only after I saw how this stuff was affecting them that I began to understand how it was affecting me. Even more importantly, only after I began to accept full responsibility for the excess of stuff in our home did things actually begin to change. After all, my husband wasn't the one bringing in most of the stuff! My kids weren't the ones who wanted to go to Target every day. Granted, we were the beneficiaries of some very generous family members — my sister-in-law, in particular, took great pleasure in showering my kids with gifts — but in those moments when I was brutally honest with myself, I began to realize that despite all my efforts to get organized, the main source of the problem was *me*.

Of course, this meant that to solve this problem, *I* was going to have to make some big changes, possibly painful ones. And *I* was going to have to fight hard to finally stop the flow, once and for all. It was going to be a battle, but it was one I was determined to win.

The first step in this battle was to *start eliminating temptation*. Simply put, I had to avoid the stores at all costs—and my advice to anyone struggling with an excess of clutter is to do the same. After all, if we don't go, we can't fill our carts with things we love. We can't be sucked into the madness. We can't fall prey to the marketing genius that works overtime to determine how to get us to fill those carts.

And make no mistake, all those stores know *exactly* how to get us to buy more. Look at the "Buy 3, Get 1 Free" promotions at your favorite bath & body shop, or the one-day sales at the local department store, or the extra discounts when you open a store credit card pretty much everywhere, or the shopping apps and coupons and limited-time offers. None of those offers—or the hundreds more just like them—are created to help us poor consumers save money. All are created to entice us to buy more.

It doesn't stop there. Every single aspect of the retail experience—from the oversized shopping carts to the layout of the store and the placement of key items at eye level to the smells and sounds and imagery—are carefully planned and executed with military-like precision to ensure every shopper spends as much time and money in their store as possible and walks out with far more stuff than we actually need.

It's not only the physical retail stores that conspire against us. Online retailers work just as hard to get us to spend just a little more. There's free shipping with a minimum purchase, daily deal sites with a new can't-miss offer happening almost every hour, one-click checkouts, bigger "Buy" buttons, and Internet cookies that let Google know exactly where we've been and what we like so they can be sure to show us those same advertisements over and over again.

Charles Duhigg, in *The Power of Habit*, explains in great detail the lengths to which my favorite store—Target—goes to track its customers and secure more sales.[3] At their headquarters in Minneapolis, they've got an entire team of statisticians who have been hired for the sole purpose of predicting the behavior of their customers, based on the vast quantities of data collected every single day. At Target, every shopper is assigned their own "Guest ID," which is connected to them through credit cards, coupons, and other trackable behaviors. Target then uses that data to figure out exactly how to market to each individual customer in the most effective way. It's pretty amazing when you think about it, but also a little scary. Essentially, Target knows what we are going to buy before *we* do. Yikes.

In my own life, retail opportunities are constantly calling my name. Despite knowing all too well the confusion, clutter, and chaos that come from filling my home with stuff I don't really need, I still want so much. I want cute clothes that flatter my figure, even if I know deep down that the only real way to feel better about the way I look is to actually lose those fifteen extra pounds I've put on over the past couple of years. I want my home to look stylish and put-together, with the same darling vignettes and displays I drool over on Pinterest, even when I know decorative vignettes only ever end up driving me crazy because my brain functions better when surfaces are clear. I want my kids to have a closet full of adorable outfits, even when I know they only want to wear the same mismatched princess shirt and striped leggings every single day.

I know I'm not alone.

Deep down, we all know stuff won't solve our problems. We *know* that. Different clothes won't make us thinner. More pretty accessories won't make our homes feel cozier. Bigger wardrobes won't make our kids happier or even make them want to wear something new. A fantastic deal — no matter how impressive the discount — won't *actually* save us money. And yet, when we walk into a store and see those things hanging there or sitting on the eye-level end cap, calling our names and painting that vision — however misguided — of how things *could* be, promising hope — however false — of the perfect life, we find it almost impossible to resist.

And so the only option for those of us who are, like me, irresistibly drawn to the promise of "what if this is the thing that changes every-thing," and someone who loves the unmatched thrill of a smoking-hot deal — is to avoid that temptation as much as possible and stay far, far away. For me, this meant no more quick trips to the craft store or Saturday afternoon strolls around the mall just to pass the time. It also meant unfollowing and unsubscribing to many daily deal sites online. After all, if I don't know about the deals, I don't know what I'm missing. For others, it may mean avoiding consignment shops, Goodwill, or garage sales. It's not really about how we much we spend or even about whether or not we can afford it, but about eliminating the temptation to fill our life with things we don't really need, regard-less of the price tag. The best and easiest solution is to just not go.

Of course, avoiding the stores completely is not always entirely possible. Thus, the second step in this battle to stop the flow is to *always stick to the essentials*. While we can avoid the stores most of the time, we do need to buy stuff sometimes, and this is when we have to be the most vigilant, because when we let down our guard, the stuff creeps back in. After all, the mindless purchases are what kill us — the harmless extras that slip into our carts with easy justification.

It's just one candle. And it's on sale. And it smells so good!

This top is on clearance — 90 percent off! What a great deal!

I've been wanting to read this book for a while now, and I'm going on vacation in a couple of weeks. I might as well get it now.

This nail polish is so pretty. I haven't done my nails in a while, and this would be the perfect pick-me-up.

Wow, this journal is marked down to $1.50! I know I can use this someday.

It's been such a hard week. I would just love to have something new.

These would be the perfect bins to finally organize my craft supplies.

Christmas is right around the corner.

This is so cute.

I work hard. I deserve to buy what I want.

There's only one left. It might be gone next time I come back.

I've been looking for something like this for so long!

My husband would love this. Maybe it will make him forget about that fight.

My kids would love this. And it would keep them entertained.

My sister would love this. Her birthday's coming up.

I love this.

It doesn't take much to break down those defenses, but by committing ahead of time to stick only to the essentials and buy only what's necessary, we can make sure our "quick errands" don't turn into a free-for-all. For some of us, simply making a list and committing to stick to it may be sufficient. Our willpower is strong, as long as we've got that list in front of us to focus on. For others of us, more drastic measures might be in order. If you find yourself slipping time and time again, consider bringing only a set amount of cash along — just enough for the items you need and no more. Or call for reinforcements and bring along a friend, sibling, or spouse who is willing to hold you accountable.

Fighting every day to prevent new stuff from coming in is the only way to really win the battle against clutter. Even the biggest closets and a full-size basement will fill up eventually. The only way to become unstuffed is to stop the flow.

Reduce by Ruthlessly Purging

They say opposites attract, and that was never so true as in the case of my husband and me. Oh, my. We are different in pretty much every way imaginable! Chuck's an engineer; I'm a writer. He likes meat; I like vegetables. He likes logic and reason; I prefer to go by feel and instinct. He likes to play it safe; I'm a risk taker. He likes to take things one day at a time; I like to plan ahead. He likes stability; I like goals. He wants to stay home; I love to travel. He's an extrovert in social situations and will easily make his way around a room; I'm much more introverted, preferring to first be introduced (usually by him). He likes variety; I like routine. He loves to relax; I love to work and am always on the go. He's meticulous about details; I'm quick and get things done, however imperfectly. He's a saver; I'm a spender. He *hates* to shop and would never set foot in another store ever again if he could avoid it; I ... well, I think we've already established that shopping comes about as naturally to me as breathing.

It has taken us almost ten years of marriage to figure out that our many, many, *many* differences are not necessarily a bad thing. To be sure, we've had our fair share of knock-down-drag-out fights over the years (yes, the one character trait we definitely share is our stubbornness), but over time, we have learned—and are still learning—how to appreciate the balance we bring to each other's lives. Yes, it does take some serious effort to learn how to compromise, but we've usually found that our greatest successes as a family come from the combination of both our strengths.

Given our history of differences, it should be no surprise that our approach to clearing the clutter is quite different as well. You see, while I *love* to bring in new things, I am also just as happy—sometimes even more so—to see them go. I am not really attached to objects, and in all honesty, I'm not that sentimental, at least not when it comes to *stuff*. Chuck, on the other hand, is *extremely* sentimental. Where I see an old ratty T-shirt that needs to be tossed, he sees a week spent building a house in Costa Rica with Habitat for Humanity. His memories are tied to the objects.

Furthermore, he's also very practical, and he really, really, *really* hates waste of any kind. To him, buying new stuff just to turn around and give away old stuff is the epitome of waste. He's not wrong.

But do you see our problem? We've got one spouse (me) who loves to shop, bringing new stuff in all the time, and another spouse (Chuck) who hates waste, refusing to let any of it go. The house becomes a black hole of *stuff*. Once something comes in, it can never, ever leave.

So what's the solution?

In our case, the first step toward resolution was something we've already discussed — I had to commit to fighting the flow and not bring new stuff in. I had to take full ownership of the fact that the source of the stuff problem we were facing was not Chuck's unwillingness to let anything go.

The source of the problem was me.

Once I was finally willing to come clean and admit the problem and change my ways, I discovered that Chuck was much more ready for a change as well. I learned that the reason he was so reluctant to let anything go was because he knew I'd just go out and find something new to take its place. Once he felt confident that the flow really had been stopped for good, he was ready to begin the process of ruthlessly purging the excess of stuff we had accumulated.

Together we made a goal to get rid of 75 percent of our stuff and to keep only the 25 percent we absolutely needed or absolutely loved. We are still working toward this goal because, in all honesty, unstuffing tends to be a slow process full of starts and stops, of backtracking and interruptions. We know we'll get unstuffed eventually, even if it takes us a while. The important thing is that we keep moving forward.

As we work toward drastically reducing the amount of stuff in our home, we've adopted some important guidelines for how and what we purge. First, we've tried to focus on only one area of our home at a time. We have discovered the hard way that decluttering can quickly and easily become overwhelming if we try to tackle too much at once, so we often break it down into small manageable bites — a drawer here, a closet there, one small section of the garage, one cupboard in the kitchen. Second, as we go through these areas, we try to *keep only that which is currently useful, despite who gave it to us and despite how much it cost.* If we haven't used it over the past two years, chances are we're not going to use it again. Third, once we've determined that something needs to go, we try to get rid of it as quickly as possible, whether that means selling it, donating it, or throwing it away. Items that linger end up coming back; the best solution is to get it out *fast.*

Your number might not be 75 percent, but chances are, if you are reading this book, it's significant. How much would you need to reduce to become truly unstuffed? Twenty-five percent? Fifty percent? More? Together with your spouse, establish a number and make it your goal. Then, one project at a time, begin to ruthlessly purge all those items that are not currently useful, regardless of who gave them to you and how much they cost. Sell, donate, toss — do whatever you need to do, but get it out quickly and get it out for good.

One helpful way to tackle your clutter in small doses is to download the Unstuffed app (get it at www.UnstuffedApp.com), which will give you one quick decluttering task for each day. Of course, if you are worried that tackling your clutter in small doses means you might never actually get a handle on it, you might also want to consider what I like to call a "blast start" — a shock to your system that can help kick off your new unstuffed mentality. If that's the case, I recommend following the Unstuffed Weekend Challenge plan outlined at the end of this chapter — it is definitely a game changer!

Establish Strict Limits

A few years ago, I was reading my friend Edie's blog, *Life in Grace*, and became totally inspired by one of her posts on closet organization. In it, she talked about her thin velvet hangers and how much she loved them. I instantly decided that the solution to my own lack of closet organization was better hangers, and off I went (to Target, of course) to procure some magical velvet hangers of my own. Of course, when I got to the store, I quickly realized that replacing all of the 150 or so cheap plastic hangers in my closet would cost a small fortune. Thus, I bought one box of forty hangers and developed a new plan.

Rather than buying new expensive hangers to hang a whole closet full of clothes I wasn't sure I even liked that much — many of which were outdated, didn't fit right, or were purchased simply because they were a great deal—I would instead pare down my wardrobe to include only the forty items I liked best. After all, what was the point of keeping clothes I never wore? One by one, I sifted through every single item in my closet, keeping only those pieces that were in great shape, that fit perfectly, that were flattering in shape and color, and that made me feel beautiful.

Surprisingly enough, it wasn't that hard to determine which clothes stayed and which ones had to go, so very few items ended up in the "maybe" pile. Faced with such a strict limit, I found that prioritizing and purging became much easier. It became immediately obvious which things I loved and which ones I could live without.

The transformation was instant and completely astounding. Although my wardrobe was now a quarter of the size that it had been, it actually felt much bigger—huge, even. Opening my closet door went from being an exercise in frustration, always feeling like I had absolutely nothing to wear, to having so many lovely choices that it was hard to narrow it down. Better yet, it was a breeze to keep it neat and organized.

Afraid to actually get rid of so many clothes all at once, I packed the remains of my forty-hanger purge in four large plastic bins, which we packed away in a forgotten corner of the garage. A year later, I hadn't missed a single thing. Not one. I was actually much happier with far less.

Now when I do consider buying something new, I know it means something else will have to go. The forty-hanger limit forces me to be selective and ultrachoosy. It is much easier to say no to that so-so top on the bargain rack when I know bringing it home will mean saying good-bye to a piece I actually love. All future purchases are held to a much higher standard, which, in the long run, saves me time, aggravation, and money.

We live in an era of abundance and excess, where the message that gets played over and over again, in every advertisement, every magazine, and every television show, is that no matter what we have or how much we have, it's not quite enough. It has unleashed an insatiable appetite in many of us, one we inadvertently pass on to our kids as well. The prevailing message is that if one is good, ten is better. If we like it, we need more. If there's a new one available, it's time for an update. This pattern of thinking is so ingrained in our psyche that we think almost nothing of it. Of course we need something new. Of course we need more.

But we don't.

Adopting a strict limit policy forces us to change our thinking. It reminds us of the fundamental truth that our consumer-driven society so desperately wants us to forget:

We already have enough.

This strict limit principle can easily be applied to almost every area of our lives, whether it be our dishes, kids' toys, books, video games, towels, socks, shoes, tools, craft supplies, candles, picture frames, pillows, makeup, jewelry, accessories, kitchen gadgets, or any other item we tend to buy in excess of what we actually need. There are even some minimalists who have taken this idea to the extreme, allowing no more than one hundred possessions — including everything from furniture to clothing to toiletries and dishes — in their entire house. While limiting yourself to one hundred items may be a bit extreme, setting your own strict limits can really help cut out the excess and make you think twice about bringing new things back in.

Emphasize Quality over Quantity

When my mother-in-law, Marie, died a few years ago, we inherited some of the furniture from the house she had lived in for more than fifty years. My very favorite pieces were a set of two mid-century modern chairs she kept in her living room. Marie loved those chairs, and for fifty years, she sat in them nearly every single day. When I look at those chairs, I can't help but think of her sitting in them, of the thousands of books she must have read there, and of the hundreds of family gatherings they hosted. I smile thinking about what those chairs have seen, but I also can't help but marvel. Because those chairs, although they are more than fifty years old, and although they were used every single day for those fifty years, still look almost brand-new. In fact, compared to the rough state of our scratched-up couch and chipped coffee table, those chairs are probably the best-looking pieces of furniture in our living room.

They just don't make things like that anymore.

High-quality merchandise is one of those things we hardly think about in this day and age, especially those of us who are extremely budget-conscious or interested in getting things as cheaply as possible. We are so inundated with a never-ending flow of ultracheap, foreign-made, poorly constructed junk that we think almost nothing of toys that break after a few days or clothing that falls apart after a season of wear. We buy too much stuff because it is inexpensive and readily available, when we could — and should — be taking a totally different kind of approach.

First, it is important to *choose long-term values over short-term bargains*. Adopting this sort of philosophy means taking a totally different look at how we consume. Instead of being swayed to make a purchase because it is a good deal or a great price, we must look at the long-term value of everything we buy, asking, *How will this item enrich my life over the next year, five years, or ten years?* Of course, this doesn't mean we spend whatever we want and only ever buy the most expensive items, but it does mean that sometimes paying a little more for something that will add long-term value to our lives is a much smarter approach.

Second, *invest in genuine quality instead of a quick fix*. Emergencies sometimes make us desperate, which in turn clouds our judgment. The toaster breaks, and we need a new one as quickly and cheaply as possible. Even so, if we can take a step back and look at the bigger picture, we will see that it is better to spend a little more money to purchase one quality piece that will stand the test of time than to have to replace a cheap, poorly made item again and again.

This means paying attention to where things are made, as well as how they are made. It means reading reviews and doing extra research before jumping in. Most importantly, it means no longer buying in to our instant gratification, throwaway culture that says it is better to have something cheap and now than to wait a little longer for something that will last.

For those of us who struggle with too much stuff, even the biggest basement won't be large enough to contain it all. Because at the heart of the matter, the problem is not the size of our closets; it is *us* — and more storage space is not the solution. Instead, we have to diligently fight the flow and truly commit to stop bringing in more. And then, once we've committed, we need to drastically reduce by ruthlessly purging the excess we've already brought in. From there, we need to set strict limits in order to hold ourselves accountable, and begin to emphasize quality over quantity. Changing our mind-set will change our actions, which in turn will be the start of becoming unstuffed.

THE UNSTUFFED WEEKEND CHALLENGE

While becoming truly unstuffed may be a long process best tackled in small doses, something can definitely be said for making a dramatic impact all at one time. Sometimes a big shock to your system can be exactly the thing that jump-starts a lasting change. If you feel like you have been drowning in clutter for too long and are ready to get serious about becoming unstuffed, consider kicking off your journey with a big weekend purge.

Here's how it works: For two and a half days, beginning on a Friday afternoon and ending on a Sunday evening, you and your family will do nothing but clear the clutter and work to transform every inch of your space. It will be a *lot* of work, and it will be physically and emotionally exhausting. But in the end it will be worth it.

Please note that this is not a project to be taken lightly, and it will require some forethought and preplanning in order to make the best use of your time and to maximize your efforts. It will also require a total commitment from every single member of your family. Every single one of you will need to be in it to win it, or you will risk giving up and dropping out when the going gets rough (which it will).

For those of you who are ready, the following plan and schedule will help you prepare and structure your plan of attack. You may have to tailor it to fit the specific needs of your own home and family, but this is a great place to start. Good luck!

How to Prepare

1. **Commit to the project.** Talk about it as family, and especially as husband and wife. Pray about it. Be honest with each other and with yourselves. Are you really ready to see the excess stuff go? Does the thought of making

this change make you feel anxious, angry, or scared? What are you hoping to gain from this exercise? Are you fully willing to give up one weekend of your life to make it happen?

2. **Assemble your team.** Many hands make light work! You might invite family members or friends to help with certain tasks or hire a teenager to take photos of things you would like to sell, drive boxes to the donation center, or help with some of the deep cleaning. As you read through the list of tasks, think of ways to divide and conquer the work.

3. **Clear your schedule.** Pick a weekend with nothing going on, and block out the entire time. This means no birthday parties, no sporting events (not even on television), no nothing. Decline any invitations or opportunities that come up. For this weekend only, the rest of the world does not exist.

4. **Arrange for child care.** If your kids are older, they should plan to help, which means clearing their schedule as well. If they are too young to help and need constant supervision, you will need to arrange for child care for the entire weekend—at a place away from home, if possible. Can they stay with a friend or grandparent for the weekend? If relatives are not an option, consider swapping weekends with another family that wants to do this same challenge. (Determine whether your child is old enough to participate by reading through the plan—as the parent you will know whether they are mature enough to tackle the required tasks. This will vary a lot from child to child.)

5. **Plan for meals.** You won't want to waste time and energy worrying about what to cook or making more work for yourself in the kitchen. Take the time to preplan easy, mess-free meals that only need to be heated up and

don't create any mess. You can purchase frozen meals, spend an afternoon creating your own freezer meals, or plan to pick up a few meals from a grocery deli or fast-food place. Consider using disposable plates and cutlery for the weekend, and make sure you have healthy, high-protein snacks on hand to keep your energy levels up.

6. **Choose a donation location.** Decide where you would like to donate your excess (hint: find the closest!), and look up their donation drop-off hours. A receipt is necessary if you plan to itemize your deductions on your income tax form (if you use the standard deduction, you cannot obtain tax credit for your donations). However, keep in mind that for tax purposes you will be required to make a list of your donated items and their fair market values in order to claim your deduction and get your receipt—a tedious step that could break the momentum you're trying to achieve this weekend.

7. **Gather your supplies.** Avoid wasting precious time during your weekend by gathering the necessary tools and supplies ahead of time. Here are some things you will most likely need:
   - heavy-duty trash bags
   - empty boxes (lots!)
   - basic tools—a hammer, flat and Phillips head screw-drivers, a tape measure
   - laundry baskets
   - a set number of hangers per family member (I like forty)
   - a label maker (optional)
   - assorted bins and baskets (optional)
   - Command adhesive hooks (optional)
   - garage shelving (optional)

The Plan

Don't forget to share pictures of your progress on social media throughout the weekend, using hashtag *#unstuffedchallenge*.

Friday

5:00 p.m. — Initial Blitz

Set the timer for ninety minutes. Turn on some high-energy music that everyone likes. Give every family member a large garbage bag and a large box, and have everyone begin in a different room, but each working their way around the entire house, clearing out the obvious clutter and garbage. Anything salvageable should be placed in boxes for donation; anything broken or worthless goes straight in the trash. If you have several items of value, you might also want to consider designating one box as a "to be sold" box, but keep in mind that this will mean extra work for your family.

Family members should use the following criteria to assess each item:

- *Do we use it? (If no, it should go.)*
- *Have we used it in the past eighteen months? (If no, it should go.)*
- *Do we like it? (If no, it should go.)*
- *Is it in good condition or good working order? (If no, it should go.)*

Remind everyone that this is a time to be both ruthless and fast. Work on filling your boxes and bags as quickly as possible, and if they fill up, grab more. There is no limit to how much you can get rid of in this first blast—the more, the better! The objective is to quickly clear as much as possible and to give yourselves a big win right out of the gate. This will help motivate all of you to do even more.

6:30 p.m. — Dinner

Set the timer for thirty minutes. Share a quick and easy meal. Use disposable dinnerware to save time cleaning up. Over dinner, discuss the first exercise and how you felt afterward. Was it harder or easier than you thought it would be? Were you surprised at how much you were able to clear out in a short amount of time?

7:00 p.m. — Living Room Purge

Set the timer for seventy-five minutes. As a family, work together to purge any remaining clutter and garbage in your living room areas. Put any items that belong elsewhere in a laundry basket to be put away. Sort through DVDs, CDs, books, knickknacks, and any other collections that have gathered in this room. Consider getting rid of throw pillows and anything else in the room that you don't love. With ten minutes left on the timer, quickly vacuum, dust, and put away laundry basket items.

8:15 p.m. — Break

Take fifteen minutes to stretch, get a drink, or go to the bathroom.

8:30 p.m. — Closet Purge

Set the timer for ninety minutes. Each family member should take this time to clear out his or her closet, removing every single item, then paring it down to the bare essentials. (Be sure to snap a "before" picture ahead of time!) Use this time to be absolutely ruthless in your purging efforts. Keep only those items that fit well, that are in good condition, and that you actually like to wear. Throw away items that are not salvageable; collect the rest in a box for donations. Limit the items you keep to a predetermined number of hangers—this will help you evaluate and prioritize even more. Hang hooks for things like coats, purses, and belts, if necessary.

10:00 p.m.—Finish Up

Load into your car all the boxes of donation items you've collected so far. Examine any items you've designated to sell and determine whether it is worth the time and trouble to sell them (hint: most of the time, it's *not* worth the trouble).

Saturday

6:45 a.m.—Wash Sheets

Clear the sheets from your bed and from your kids' beds and start a load of sheets. If you can't fit everything into one load, wash your master bedroom sheets first.

7:00 a.m.—Post Items for Sale and/or Drop Off Donations

Take pictures of any items you want to sell and post them on Craigslist or a local Facebook online garage sale group. Make sure your photos are in focus, with lots of natural lighting, and price them to sell quickly. Take a picture of your first load and then deliver all the boxes of donation items from the day before to your local thrift store or donation center. DO THIS ASAP! It is imperative that you get the items *out* of your house as quickly as possible. If the donation center opens later in the day, designate the earliest possible time to make your drop-off, perhaps during the 10:30 a.m. break time.

8:30 a.m. — Breakfast

Enjoy a protein-packed power breakfast—you're going to need lots of energy for today! Use disposable dinnerware to save time cleaning up. Over breakfast, discuss your plan of action for the day. (Also, be sure to transfer your sheets to the dryer and start another load, if necessary!)

9:00 a.m. — Bathrooms

Set the timer for ninety minutes. Choose whether you want to work together or divide and conquer. You will need a large garbage bag and a box for donations. Quickly work your way through each drawer and cabinet, tossing any products that have expired or that you no longer use, as well as excess accessories and other bathroom goods. Be ruthless and quick—try not to spend time agonizing; just get rid of anything you don't actually use. Remove excess towels too, especially any that are frayed or worn. Wipe down drawers and shelves; then return items that you are keeping in a neat and orderly fashion. Hang hooks for towels if you don't already have them. Spend the last ten to fifteen minutes wiping down the counters, mirrors, and toilet and sweeping or mopping the floors.

10:30 a.m. — Break

Take fifteen minutes to stretch, get a drink, or go to the bathroom. Remove sheets from the dryer; transfer a second load to the dryer, if necessary.

10:45 a.m. — Master Bedroom

While your closets and bathrooms might now be clean and organized, your bedroom itself may still need some work to become the relaxing, clutter-free haven you've always dreamed of. Set the timer for ninety minutes. Start by making the bed with your nice clean sheets. Clear your surfaces—dressers, desks, and tables—of all clutter, getting rid of anything and everything that you don't use regularly, that doesn't work, or that you don't absolutely love. Collect in a laundry basket any items that belong elsewhere. Go through your drawers and purge any remaining clothing, using the same criteria you used in your closet, keeping only the items that fit well, are in good condition, and you like wearing. Once again, be completely ruthless! Spend the last ten minutes dusting, vacuuming, and returning items to their proper homes.

12:15 p.m. — Lunch

Set the timer for forty-five minutes. Share another quick and easy meal. Use disposable dinnerware to save time cleaning up.

1:00 p.m. — Kitchen and Dining Area, Part 1

Set the timer for ninety minutes. This will be the purging portion of this task, so be ready to do some serious eliminating; have a heavy-duty garbage bag and several boxes ready. Start with the fridge and freezer, throwing out anything that has been open for too long or has passed its expiration date. Do this as quickly as possible, without really thinking or agonizing over it too much. Repeat the process for the pantry and then move on to the nonfood items—pots, pans, baking supplies, utensils, dishes, and so on. Put everything on the counter so you can see it all. Get rid of multiples and anything you don't use. Again, be ruthless. If you don't use it, why is it there? Go through every cupboard and drawer, and don't stop until all the clutter has been cleared. If necessary, repeat this process for the dining room hutch or sideboard. Remember, you have only ninety minutes for this task, so you need to be efficient!

2:30 p.m.—Break

Take fifteen minutes to stretch, get a drink, or go to the bathroom.

2:45 p.m.—Kitchen and Dining Area, Part 2

Set the timer for ninety minutes. This will be the restoration portion of this task—the part where you put it all back together. Wipe down all the cleared-out cabinets and drawers, and put back into their homes in an orderly fashion all the kitchen and dining wares you will be keeping. Once the counters have been cleared, remove all the remaining food from the pantry, wipe down shelves, and return food in an orderly fashion. Repeat this process with the refrigerator, removing everything, wiping down shelves thoroughly, and returning food. Finish by cleaning any dirty dishes, wiping down the sink, wiping down the kitchen counters, and then sweeping or mopping the floors.

4:15 p.m.—Break

Take fifteen minutes to stretch, get a drink, or go to the bathroom.

4:30 p.m.—Kids' Rooms and Closets

Set the timer for ninety minutes. If your kids are older and have already been helping with this challenge, then this will be your time to inspect the work they've done and see if you can help them. If your kids are young and haven't helped, this will be your time to clear their clutter and organize their closets, following the same guidelines you used for your own closet and bedroom. In either case, be sure to start by making the beds with those fresh, clean sheets!

6:00 p.m. — Post Items for Sale and/or Drop Off Donations

Take pictures of any items you want to sell and post them on Craigslist or a local Facebook online garage sale group. Make sure your photos are in focus, with lots of natural lighting, and price them to sell quickly. Take a picture of your second load and then deliver all the boxes of donation items to your local thrift store or donation center. (Make sure the donation center is open this late.) While you are out, pick up dinner at a grocery deli or fast-food place.

6:30 p.m. — Dinner

Set the timer for sixty minutes. Over dinner, discuss everything you've managed to accomplish so far—clearing the clutter in the living room, bedrooms, bathroom, and kitchen. Are you happy with your progress?

7:30 p.m. — Basement or Playroom

Set the timer for ninety minutes. As a family, work together to purge out any remaining clutter and garbage in your basement or playroom. Place into a laundry basket any items that belong elsewhere to be put in their proper place. Sort through toys, games, holiday decorations, and any other collections that have gathered in this room. Get rid of anything that you don't use, that doesn't work, or that you don't love. Be absolutely ruthless with what you get rid of, especially toys! With ten minutes left on the timer, quickly vacuum, dust, and put away laundry basket items.

9:00 p.m. — Finish Up

Use this time to finish up any projects you didn't have time to complete, or simply take a few minutes to relax. Take a hot shower. Have a drink or a cup of tea. You worked hard today—great job!

Sunday

Morning—Rest and Church

You may feel a bit sore from yesterday's physical work. Relish the feeling, especially the sense of a job well-done! Enjoy a relaxing breakfast with your family. Over breakfast or lunch, discuss your plan of action for the afternoon. Try to catch an early church service if you want to get an early start on the garage—you might need the extra time!

12:30 p.m.—Garage, Part 1

If you are anything like my husband and me, no single area of your home invokes more terror than the garage! But now that you are practically an old pro at decluttering, it is finally time to tackle this dreaded zone head-on. Set the timer for ninety minutes and then focus for this time period on purging as much as you can, as quickly as you can. Begin moving everything OUT of the garage and onto the driveway, purging as you go. Fill up your collection boxes and garbage bags with anything that does not get used, that doesn't work, and that you don't love. Also get rid of anything that is garbage—old paint cans, broken tools, empty containers, and so on. Once again, you have only ninety minutes for this task, so move quickly! Your goal is to have the entire garage cleared out by the time the buzzer sounds.

2:00 p.m.—Break

Take fifteen minutes to stretch, get a drink, or go to the bathroom.

2:15 p.m. — Garage, Part 2

Set the timer for ninety minutes. Once the garage has been completely cleared and swept clean of dirt and debris, it is time to work on creating practical storage solutions for the items you will be keeping. Set up some heavy-duty shelving if it's not there already, and install a few heavy-duty hooks for hanging items. Return items to the garage, purging additional items as you go. With every item you bring back, ask yourself the following questions: *Do I really use this? Does it work? Do I really like it and want it?* If the answer to any of them is no, then let it go.

3:45 p.m. — Break

Take fifteen minutes to stretch, get a drink, or go to the bathroom.

4:00 p.m. — Final Pass

Set the timer for ninety minutes. This is your time to tackle any areas specific to your home that weren't covered in this plan or to go back and finish any areas you weren't quite able to complete in the allotted amount of time. This is also your time to go through the entire house one more time to see if there is anything else you can get rid of. Remember—the more stuff you have, the more work it creates for you. If you don't love it and it doesn't add value to your life, why are you hanging on to it?

5:30 p.m. — Finish Up

Load all of today's boxes of donation items into the car and, if possible, deliver them to the nearest donation center. Consider going out to dinner to celebrate your accomplishment. You did it. Way to go!

three

Kids

The Stuff Just Keeps Coming

Tell me and I forget; teach me and I may remember;
involve me and I learn.

Benjamin Franklin

It has now been more than three years since that fateful moment when I packed up all my kids' toys and inadvertently kicked off a toy-free revolution. The blog post I wrote about the incident went viral online many times over, receiving millions of page views, hundreds of thousands of shares, and thousands of comments and letters, ranging from parents who were inspired to do the same, to those who dismissed me as a control freak, to those who threatened to call the authorities since I was clearly causing lasting psychological damage to my poor, deprived, toyless children. The majority of parents who read the post seemed to relate to my frustration, and most even cheered me on, but there were also quite a few who thought I was downright cruel and possibly even borderline abusive. The debate still rages on today. (To read the original post, visit www.LivingWellSpendingLess.com/toys.)

For the most part, I have learned to tune it out.

It's not that I don't care what others have to say, or even that I think I made the right call and that those who would criticize me are completely wrong. On the contrary, my critics have brought up some valid points. I'm also thrilled that other parents have found hope and inspiration from reading about our experience—which is exactly why I shared it in the first place. In fact, that is the reason I bother sharing *any* of our own experiences. But quite honestly, we've moved on.

You see, while taking away my kids' toys was definitely an important moment in our lives and a turning point for our family, it was only one of many, many moments, both good and bad. And while in the years since, we have tried to be a lot more proactive about keeping our girls' pile of books and clothes and toys and games and keepsakes and papers to a minimum, they still have *a lot*—far more than they need and far more than I would like.

Because as every parent knows, with kids, the stuff just keeps coming.

It's endless.

Every birthday invitation means another goodie bag full of cheap plastic garbage. A good day at school ends with a prize from the treasure box. The next-door neighbor drops off a box of toys their own kids are no longer playing with, or a sweet auntie sends a care package full of goodies just because. Every holiday brings its own pile—Christmas presents, Easter baskets, Valentine's treats, birthday gifts. New clothes because the old ones wear out and become play clothes but still stick around. And then there's the artwork and crafts and projects. And the papers. Oh, the papers.

It's endless.

Or maybe it's just *my* kids who have seemingly become a bottomless source of stuff. In any case, the reality is that our completely toy-free environment—the one I wrote about in that viral blog post—was only temporary. The stuff keeps coming back. And as my daughters get older, they are also much more sentimental and interested in hanging on to their things. They now remember where certain items came from and who their gifts are from. Their special trinkets may not have much value to *me*, but they certainly mean something to *them*. What I see as clutter, they see as treasure.

But that doesn't mean I don't keep trying or that we haven't looked for ways to strike a balance between letting our kids hold on to things they truly love and appreciate and preventing our home from becoming a kid-clutter free-for-all. I'm not sure we will ever get it exactly right, but over the years, we have stumbled upon a few helpful strategies that let all of us keep our sanity in the midst of this battle. In the end, just like with my own clutter, it comes down to getting FREE of clutter: **F**ighting the flow, **R**uthlessly purging, **E**stablishing limits, and **E**mphasizing quality over quantity. Additionally, fighting the battle of stuff *alongside* our kids, rather than only *for* them, will also help them learn vitally important life lessons about the value of money, the reality of hard work (which includes caring for stuff!), and the responsibility of stewarding our resources wisely. It's a big job, I admit—one that wears me out sometimes. Let's face it, parenting is hard work! But the alternative—entitled, spoiled kids who can't fend for themselves and who are drowning in a sea of stuff they don't need—isn't something I'm willing to settle for.

Fighting the Culture of Consumerism

I can remember that Christmas like it was yesterday. The year was 1985. I was seven years old, and there was only one thing I really wanted, something I wanted more than I had ever wanted anything before in my short little life.

A Cabbage Patch doll.

My heart was set on it, and I *longed* for that doll. I wanted it so bad I could practically feel it in my arms. I spent hours daydreaming about what she would look like, what color her yarn hair would be, what adorable little outfit she'd be wearing, what color eyes she'd have, whether or not she'd have a tooth, and when her birthday would be. I didn't really have a preference; all I knew was that if I didn't get one, my life would be over.

Conversations with the other girls at school revolved around our speculations. I was far from the only girl in my class wishing and hoping for one of these magical dolls. News stories that year revolved around the growing frenzy, with near stampedes in the toy stores as people tried to get their hands on one. And every morning in the weeks before Christmas, I'd run downstairs to check the ever-growing pile of presents under the tree, just to see if any new boxes had my name on it.

And then one morning, there it was — a new box with my name on it. There could be no mistaking that telltale trapezoid shape, and it had *my* name on it. Mine.

I'm sure it was only a week at the most, but at the time it felt like *years* waiting for the moment to finally arrive. I thought I might die from the suspense. My stomach was in knots.

And then it was Christmas Eve. I was practically beside myself waiting for nightfall, and then I could hardly eat my dinner, knowing what was going to happen next. When was it going to be time? When dinner was over, my family headed toward the living room — my mom and dad; two college-aged brothers, Mark and Paul; my older sister, Beth; and little brother, Joel. Both sets of grandparents were there too — my mom's stoic Dutch immigrant parents and my dad's parents as well, who had recently retired and just moved into town.

Finally it was time for gifts.

As the youngest, Joel got to go first. To this day, I have no idea what he got. All I could see, all I could think about, was that box. My Cabbage Patch doll. I just wanted her in my arms.

Unwrapping was a blur and then there she was, in my arms, just like I had dreamed about. Andi Harrietta, born in the Cabbage Patch on November 1. She had twinkly green eyes, brown pigtail braids, a dimpled cheek, a single tooth, and a cute little yellow flowered onesie, with white socks and white shoes. She was perfect. And she was all mine.

And then something happened.

My grandma, the Dutch one, asked to look at her.

"Rooshie," she said, in her thick Dutch accent, "yet me zee dat doll."

I ran over to her, thrilled to be able to share my excitement. She took the doll in her hands and looked it over closely.

"Ach ach ach, dit is vreselijk, vreselijk, kleine jongens," she said. *"Wat een lelijk dolletje!"*

Although I didn't speak much Dutch at the time, there was no mistaking her tone. She thought my precious Cabbage Patch doll was terrible — the ugliest doll she had ever seen. For a moment I was crushed, but then more presents were opened, and those brutally honest words were soon forgotten. It wasn't until many years later, after the Cabbage Patch buzz had died down and the media had moved on to the next big thing, that I realized my grandmother had been right.

They are not very attractive dolls.

And as much as I loved my doll (and I did love her for many years), the only reason I really wanted a Cabbage Patch doll so badly was because everyone else did too. Every other commercial on Saturday morning hammered in the message that my life would practically be over if I didn't have a doll to call my own. Even my parents, who were normally unaffected by trends, bought into the frenzy that year. This was clearly the toy to have, and they would be remiss as parents if they didn't join the stampede and come through with a doll for their daughter.

It took a wise but blunt old Dutch woman to see through all the propaganda and all the hype to call it out for what it was — nothing more than incredibly fantastic marketing for a ridiculously ugly doll.

You would think, as a society, we would have learned our lesson, but almost every year, there seems to be something new, some must-have hot toy. Remember Teddy Ruxpin? Transformers? Tickle Me Elmo? Beanie Babies? Nintendo Game Boy? Furby? Even now, the fads come and go. Lalaloopsy, LeapPad, Xbox 360, FurReal Friends, iPod Touch. According to the commercials, there is always something we can't live without.

A few years ago, in a year that will forever be known in our family as "The Year of the Rat," my sister-in-law Linda went more than a little overboard on one such fad. An elementary school principal with no children of her own, Linda *loved* lavishing gifts on my girls, her only two nieces. Because she worked with kids every day, she always knew exactly what the must-have toys of the season would be. Thus, when Zhu Zhu pets — little battery-operated wheeled hamsters — hit the scene, she was on it, ready to make sure she procured every possible piece of the Zhu Zhu habitat (all pieces sold separately), as well as every single pet available at the time. I've never seen someone more committed to a cause. She searched every local store and hunted online — and even convinced her school secretary to do the same. She got to know the store manager at the local Walmart to get an inside scoop on when the next shipments were coming in. She stood in lines and raced around like a crazy person, refusing to rest until she had claimed every piece in the entire set.

And then Christmas morning arrived, and four-year-old Maggie, with help from Auntie Linda, began the momentous task of opening all those Zhu Zhu pet packages. They spent hours unwrapping, and countless more hours setting up the habitat, a task made all the more frustrating by the fact that none of the fittings on the poorly made, cheap plastic pieces actually snapped together the way they were supposed to, which meant that everything kept falling apart. But finally — *finally* — it was time to bring out the rats — uh, I mean *hamsters* — to explore their new habitat. We all gathered around and handed Maggie the first Zhu Zhu — a pink one named Sweetie — so that she could have the thrill of turning it on and setting it into the maze for the first time.

Little Maggie excitedly flipped the switch and immediately proceeded to get her long hair completely wrapped up in the tiny axle of the hamster's wheels. After twenty minutes of yelling, crying, and haircutting, we were ready to give the hamsters another go, this time with all hair safely tied back. The whole family watched in anticipation as the little mechanical creatures began to move. For about thirty seconds, we enjoyed watching them scoot around. Until, of course, the first hamster got stuck. And then the second one couldn't make it up the hill. And the third one stopped working completely.

It was an unmitigated disaster. After four hours of setup and less than five minutes of playtime, we were done with them. I mean, so done. We packed up all the pieces and brought them to the attic, where they still reside to this day. We thought about selling them or donating them, but truthfully couldn't bear the thought of subjecting another family to the torture. So there they sit, a concrete reminder to never again fall prey to the hype. "Remember the Rats!" has become our battle cry.

This battle against the influx of stuff in our kids' lives starts at the front lines, with the very culture of consumerism we have all grown up in, a culture that has only become more demanding as time goes on. This perpetual cycle of hype has become so prevalent and pervasive that sometimes we don't even realize we've fallen for it until afterward. Advertisers and marketers are experts at this game of making us — the consumer — want what we don't already have and convincing us that one brand is better than another, one product superior to all the rest. Billions of dollars are spent every year to make sure the message comes through loud and clear, and these same marketers know that the most receptive audience they can reach are those too young to ask questions and too immature to fight back. They want a captive audience. They want the hearts and minds of our kids.

As parents, it is our job to fight back daily against this culture of consumerism and to protect our kids from being inundated with propaganda about what to buy. Proverbs 4:23 wisely tells us, "Above all else, guard your heart, for everything you do flows from it." It is our job to turn off the television sets, eliminate commercials, limit screen time, and be aware of the messages that are coming in. It is our job to have open and honest conversations about wants versus needs and to say that enough is enough, because our kids will certainly not do it themselves.

AGES AND STAGES

Battling the overflow of stuff in our kids' lives is an ongoing battle, one that requires us to work both *for* and *with* our kids to be successful not only in fighting the culture of consumerism but in ruthlessly purging, setting stricter limits, and knowing the value of money. This battle will look very different for a two-year-old than it will for a teenager. Here are some key points to work on in each stage of your child's life.

Birth–2 Years

This is where it all begins. Set up your child for success from the very start by setting strict limits for yourself and for your family members. Patterns set at this stage will continue throughout your child's life, so be purposeful about the choices you make and keep clothing, toys, and gear down to a minimum. Work on maintaining a regular routine, with a scheduled daily naptime. And begin to teach your toddler to pick up toys.

Ages 3–5

Kids at this stage can easily become overwhelmed by too many toys and choices. Consider keeping only one small bin or basket of toys available at any given time, and rotate them with other options once a week. You will have to set most of the limits and do most of the purging yourself, so once you start to feel overwhelmed with kid stuff, you might institute a one-in, one-out policy. You might also institute a kid "junk drawer," a place where you can throw all the birthday party goodies, fast-food meal toys, and other trinkets that kids accumulate at this age. (I've found you can dump this stuff later and they won't even notice, but woe unto thee if you throw it away the day they get it!) Kids at this age can start helping with basic household chores, such as picking up toys and books, dusting or wiping flat surfaces, putting their laundry in the hamper, helping to match socks, or setting or clearing the table. A regular routine is also important for this age group. If your child has stopped napping, institute an hour or two of "Quiet Time in Your Room" each day. Resist the temptation to let kids at this age spend much time watching television or playing with electronic devices such as an iPad. Not only does consuming too much media inhibit critical brain development; it also perpetuates the culture of consumerism through advertisements targeted specifically to kids. And moms, if you're done having babies, this is a great stage for purging baby paraphernalia.

Ages 6 – 9

Elementary-age kids are learning how to interact with their peers, which means they are also easily influenced by the behavior and attitudes of their friends and classmates. This means, as parents, that constant vigilance is in order. Be consistent about emphasizing your expectations and values with your kids and about working with them to set limits on their stuff and to purge when necessary, especially when they have outgrown a toy. At this age, you can give them large under-the-bed plastic boxes where they can begin to store treasured school papers and artwork, with the understanding that it is their responsibility to purge items when the box gets full. This is also the perfect age to start implementing a commission system and to start adding chores, such as taking care of pets, putting away groceries, making the bed, folding laundry, emptying the trash, sweeping the floor, vacuuming, watering the plants, and loading or unloading the dishwasher. At this stage, you may also want to consider using a chore chart.* It is still important at this stage to strictly limit screen time—experts recommend no more than an hour per day!

Ages 10–13

Tweens are even more susceptible to peer pressure, which means that as parents, this is no time to let up! Your kids will still need guidance and instruction to help make good choices, set limits, and decide what and when to purge, but you will need to allow them to start using their own judgment. Remember, they must also learn that actions have consequences, so part of your job is to let them feel the pain of their mistakes, as well as the pain of letting go. At this stage, you may want to do a big toy purge, where you help your child say good-bye to stuffed animals, toys, books, games, and costumes that no longer fit their age or interests. You may want to expand your commission system a little and help your child start budgeting more for certain expenses, such as school clothes or paying for a cell phone, perhaps giving them a certain amount of money they control. Additional chores for this age can include cleaning the kitchen, doing the laundry, washing the cars, mowing the lawn, mopping floors, babysitting siblings, packing lunches, washing windows, taking out the trash, and helping to plan and cook meals. If your child does have their own cell phone at this point, it is more than appropriate to set limits on how and when it can be used—just be sure to enforce them! One of my friends has a great rule for her kids—at home, all cell phones stay on the kitchen counter, and if her kids want to use them for any reason, they must do it at the counter.

---

*For instructions on how to access a variety of printable chore chart options, see page 219 at the back of the book.

Ages 14–18

High schoolers are little adults in training, and for the most part, they should be treated that way. Parents in this stage need to be clear about their expectations and about responsibilities. Kids at this stage need to be fully responsible for their own stuff—how much they take in, what they keep, how they take care of it, and what they get rid of, though it is the parents' task to teach them the right skills and to enforce the rules. The idea that actions have consequences will be critically important for this age group. Kids at this stage can be responsible for their own budget and should begin paying for at least some of their own expenses, such as a car, gas, insurance, entertainment, and clothing. They should also be strongly encouraged to get a part-time job. In addition, you should reinforce the idea that they will be moving out one day—and do they really want to move boxes and boxes of stuff with them? These actions may seem harsh at first, but kids who have learned to take responsibility for themselves and their belongings are generally happier, more secure, and better equipped for success than their classmates who have had everything handed to them and taken care of for them.

They don't yet have the wisdom to discern the difference between hype and reality. They need us to do it for them. And as parents, it is our job to know that *it is okay to say no.*

The fads aren't going away anytime soon, and the hype, propaganda, media frenzy, and "gotta have it now" mentality will be around for a long, long time. But we can choose to change the way we react to them. We can choose to turn off that message and refuse to be swayed. We can choose to guide our kids and teach them how to buck the trends. We can eliminate a culture of consumerism in our own lives and in the lives of our kids. We can say no to the rats.

Ruthlessly Purge

"The Year of the Rat" was a momentous Christmas for our family, not just because of the ill-fated Zhu Zhu pets. It was also the year that my sister-in-law Linda came bearing so many gifts that it literally took us all day to open them. From 7:00 a.m. until 7:00 p.m. that evening, we did nothing but open gift after gift after gift. Actually that's not *entirely* true. Maggie and Annie did nothing but open gift after gift after gift while the rest of the family watched.

At first, it was sort of sweet. We knew Linda adored our girls. Her love language was gifts, and this was her way of showing them how much she cared. And it was all *very* nice stuff. There was an Ariel vanity and a three-story KidKraft dollhouse. A Barbie motor home with a whole extended family of dolls to go with it. There were baby dolls and books and games and custom-monogrammed sleeping bags with matching teepees and stuffed animals and lots and lots of very pretty, very fancy clothes. Plus, it was her money. What was it to us if she wanted to spend it on our kids?

But as the empty boxes and bags of garbage piled up in the garage, we became more and more anxious about the situation. What were they going to do with all this stuff? How could they possibly play with it all? Where would they even wear all those dresses? And where would we possibly put it all in our three-bedroom, no-basement house? At some point, Chuck even had to leave the room because he just couldn't take it anymore.

I wish I could say we handled the situation gracefully. I wish I could say that at some quiet, appropriate moment, we pulled Linda aside and gently explained that, while we were incredibly grateful for her generosity, we just felt like this was far too much stuff for two little girls to have, and that we wanted them to be able to truly appreciate a few things rather than be overwhelmed by such a large pile. I also wish I could say we told her we knew how much she loved our girls, and that we knew she wanted what was best for them, and that we knew she would want them to grow up to be sweet, grateful girls, not bratty entitled ones, and that we were afraid that, over time, so many gifts all the time would start to lose their meaning to them. And I wish I could say that after we talked, she totally saw our point and agreed to stop going overboard, and that everything was completely perfect from there on out.

But none of that happened.

Instead, after Christmas, Linda flew back to her home in Kansas City, and we were left to deal with the mess left behind. Our New Year's resolution that year was to try to get a handle on the avalanche of stuff that was threatening to bury us alive, and so we began to sift and sort and selectively pick things to donate or sell. We figured that if Linda ever asked about a certain item, we could just tell her it was in the attic for a little while. It was a perfect plan, we decided, and Linda would never have to know.

It may very well have been a perfect plan, except for the fact that I am a blogger, and also sometimes a complete idiot. In my eagerness to share my organizing and decluttering progress with my blog readers, I triumphantly took a picture of the back of our Tahoe filled to the brim with donation items, many of which were gifts from Linda.

Ouch. Talk about ruthlessly purging!

Even now, years later, I cringe when I think about how much that picture must have hurt her. Because yes, of course she saw it, and yes, of course she was incredibly upset and offended by it. As well she should have been. It was beyond harsh.

It's a delicate tightrope to walk — this line between not wanting to hurt the ones we love and actually making effective headway in this battle against stuff. After all, none of us want to suffer casualties. Our goal is certainly not to alienate the people we love. The fact is, this process of ruthless purging will probably look different at different ages and stages of our kids' lives. Our end goal is ultimately not to make the decisions for our children, though we may have to when they are very young, but to equip them with the ability to take care of and regulate their own stuff. The older they get, the more we can teach them that if they can't take care of or don't use something, it has to go. As they get older still, we can encourage teens to purge their own piles of stuff by reminding them that they won't want to be burdened with sorting or moving them some day.

Set Limits

I know we could have avoided a lot of hurt feelings with my sister-in-law by just being honest from the get-go. But that photograph of the packed Tahoe did serve one positive purpose. It finally opened up a very honest conversation about gifts and about how we wanted to raise our kids. We finally, after apologizing profusely, were able to explain that we loved that she loved them, but that we wanted them to remember her for the time she spent with them, not for the pile of presents she brought with her when she visited. We set limits with Linda by clearly laying out our boundaries and expectations.

The change didn't happen overnight, but it did happen. Linda began to ask us about what the girls actually needed rather than go crazy buying dozens of the hottest toys around. When we home-schooled, she helped us supply our classroom with a beautiful globe and learning materials, and with our blessing, she took great pride in procuring the most elaborate Christmas and Easter dresses she could find. She also took to heart our suggestion to just spend time with them, securing her spot in their hearts as the most fun auntie on the planet. When she died of cancer a year ago, we were all devastated, but I'm so thankful that the memories my girls have are attached to *her* and not just to her stuff.

It's easy to use holidays and special occasions as an excuse for more stuff. After all, our consumer-driven culture keeps driving home the message that Christmas is all about the gifts, that Easter is all about the baskets, and that birthdays without presents are, well, just not birthdays at all. But those are all *lies*, and they are lies that we, as parents, have the power to say no to. We can say yes to the special without saying yes to the stuff. They don't have to go hand in hand.

So take the initiative to explain your limits both to your kids and to the gift givers in their lives. This can mean instituting a "no gift" policy at birthday parties or limiting Christmas gifts to a certain number. I've heard of many families who limit their gifts to three to represent the number of gifts brought by the wise men, and of others who follow a "something you want, something you need, something to wear, and something to read" policy. For birthdays, we usually give our girls a choice between going on a trip somewhere or having their friends over for a party. This could also mean sitting down with your child to decide on a reasonable number of toys or clothing—not while you are in the midst of a mess, but before you've even started, when defenses are low. Ask them point-blank: What's a reasonable number of stuffed animals or toys or shoes or shirts? Chances are, the number they choose will be less than you would have been willing to set on your own! The limit may mean instituting a policy of "one in, one out," in your home for books, toys, clothing, and other items.

It may feel awkward at first to be so clear with others about what you want for your family, but it pays off in less incoming stuff. Also, as you set limits with various gift givers in your child's life, try to pick gift ideas you know will interest the gift giver. Does your sister love to shop for clothing? Let her know what items your child has recently grown out of, or of any special events coming up that he or she may need a new outfit for. Does your grandmother prefer to keep things practical? Why not give her a list of needed school supplies? The goal is not to alienate the people who love your kids, but to instead find a way to work together for the good of your children through open communication and clearly defined limits.

Teach the Value of Money

While fighting the culture of consumerism, ruthlessly purging, and learning to set limits are all important, there is probably no single better way to fight the accumulation of stuff than to teach your children that money—and therefore hard work—goes into every single purchase. As important as it is to protect our kids from outside influences and a culture always telling us to buy more, it is equally important to teach our children the value of money so they are able to make better choices about how to spend their hard-earned cash as they get older.

The single phrase that my husband and I have begun hammering home for our kids is that *money comes from work*. We want them to understand, beyond a shadow of a doubt, that all the stuff in their life was purchased with money, and that all of that money came from our hard work. We also want them to understand that if they want stuff, they are going to have to work for it, and they are going to have to take care of it.

We've discovered that using a commission system—where our kids get paid for the work they do—is more effective at teaching this concept than simply offering them a weekly allowance where they get paid no matter what. Let me tell you, *this system works*! The closer it gets to payday, the more enthusiastic my girls become about helping out around the house. They absolutely love filling the check marks in their chore chart and then counting up their money at the end of the week. Our payday happens on Sunday night so they have all weekend to boost their payout. Their chores and pay scale are based on their age—our older daughter Maggie has a few harder tasks that can earn more money, while our younger daughter Annie simply earns a quarter per check mark. Then, when payday comes, that commission gets split into three separate envelopes—one to spend, one to save, and one to give, a system we learned about while taking Dave Ramsey's Financial Peace University class and then refined after reading Dave and his daughter Rachel Cruze's wonderful book titled *Smart Money, Smart Kids*.

Of course, teaching our kids the value of money is certainly not the only thing the chore system does. We know that as parents, the greatest gift we can give them is the ability to fend for themselves when they grow up. My husband often tells the girls, "My most important job is to make you a good grown-up."

Here are a few of the other lessons we are currently working on:

With ownership comes responsibility. For instance, owning a car means obtaining a license and insurance, following traffic rules, and keeping up with maintenance. Yet how many parents forget that children need to learn this basic lesson that with ownership comes responsibility! Owning toys means taking responsibility to pick them up and put them away. Owning clothes means putting them in the laundry to be washed or hanging them up in the closet. Owning a cell phone means protecting it from loss or damage and pitching in to pay monthly fees.

Actions have consequences. Teaching your kids that actions have consequences is a lesson that becomes very concrete when you involve their stuff. If they leave their favorite baseball glove outside, it could be ruined by rain. If they can't pick up their Legos, you'll be happy to sweep them up — into a "toy time-out" or, more drastically, into the trash! (That's a tough one to follow through on.) I'll be honest, it is *hard* to let your kids fail or to set disciplinary limits. None of us want to see our kids stumble or struggle or get hurt, but too often we become enablers for their self-destructive behavior by not allowing them to learn lessons the *hard* way — because they've refused to learn them the *easy* way.

Waiting is good for you. We now live in an Internet age of instant gratification, one that is becoming more so all the time, and sadly, far too many kids grow up thinking that if they want it, they should have it *right now*. A few years ago, I was the director of a large day spa, and I saw this all too frequently with my entry-level front desk employees, who were mostly girls in their late teens and early twenties who thought working at a spa would be fun, glamorous, and easy. I can't even tell you the number of times one would ask for a raise after just a week—or sometimes even a few days—of work. They had been so accustomed to being rewarded for nothing that they had no concept of delayed gratification. It was sad and, as an employer, extremely frustrating.

Numerous studies have demonstrated that one of the keys to success is the ability to delay gratification. And your kids will never develop that moral muscle unless you give them opportunities to flex it—by keeping them waiting!

Through our commission system, my own girls are slowly learning to wait and to save for the things they want. Each week they get a little closer to their goals, and each week they become a little more motivated to work harder. And the more time they spend working, the less time they spend wishing for something or buying junk, and they become more aware of just how much work it takes to buy what they want.

It's not all about you. Not long ago, I was stopped in my tracks by one simple but life-changing question: *What are you doing with God's money?* As a Christian, I believe that what I have is not my own. Instead, I am called to be a good steward of the resources I've been given, and just as importantly, I am called to teach my children to do the same.

I take this responsibility seriously, but in all honesty, this calling is not a burden. There is no greater joy than teaching my kids how to give! We do this in lots of different ways, especially at Christmas, and our favorite way to give is with our time, not just our money. Even so, it is important for my kids to understand that the time they have, the money they earn, and the stuff they own need to be shared. Each week, at payday, they first put a portion in their "give" envelope. And at least a few times a year, they sort through their toys and decide what they will donate to Goodwill or some other charity. They get to decide how much they will give, and they also get to pick the recipient, since at this point we are far less concerned with the particulars than that they experience the joy of giving. I'm sure our giving plan will evolve and adapt as they get older, but giving of their time, money, and belongings will always be an important part of their training to be responsible adults.

Choose contentment. While all these other concepts are important, helping my kids learn to live with a spirit of contentment is by far the most important lesson I will ever teach them. A wise person once said there are two ways to be rich — one is to have everything you want, and the other is to be satisfied with what you have. In our home, we call this our "attitude of gratitude," and the subject comes up a lot, especially when my kids start to get whiny or act entitled.

The opportunity to put these concepts into practice with our kids happens almost daily in both big and small ways. Not long ago, for instance, we decided to surprise our girls and two of their friends with a visit to Disney on Ice, which was touring nearby. We drove the forty-five minutes to Fort Myers without their having a clue about where we were going, and we kept our secret until we were in the parking lot. As the six of us walked into the arena, the girls were positively giddy with excitement. Until, of course, they spotted all the light-up wands, cotton candy, stuffed toys, and other assorted trinkets for sale. Their attitudes instantly shifted from excitement to longing.

After listening to several rounds of "please, please, pleeeeaaase can we have that, Mommy and Daddy?" we gently encouraged them to list all the things they were experiencing (getting to see princesses, having a fun sleepover with friends, and so on) rather than focusing on things we weren't buying. It completely changed their perspective, and we all had a great time. (And just in case you're wondering, yes, my husband and I sometimes have to remind each other of this too!)

As parents, teaching the value of money and the responsibility of ownership is a daily choice we have to make, and demonstrating the delay of gratification, the stewardship of our resources, and an attitude of gratitude goes right along with that. If we want our kids to live an unstuffed life, we must be willing to walk that road right along with them — and be willing to go first.

Proverbs 22:6 tells us, "Start children off on the way they should go, and even when they are old they will not turn from it." This means it is our job as parents to protect our kids from the influx of stuff, to guard their hearts and minds from the culture of consumerism that pervades our society, and to diligently teach them the value of money and the responsibility that goes along with owning stuff. It's an ongoing battle, one that won't end until they are grown, because as far as kids are concerned, the stuff just keeps coming. But don't give up, because at the end of the day, we are the parents, and we have the power to win.

LAY DOWN THE LIMITS

Depending on their age and stage, your children will need your help in determining what the limits should be in regard to their toys, games, books, keepsakes, clothing, and anything else that accumulates. Here are some concrete ways you can set those limits.

Use a box, basket, shelf, drawer, or cupboard to draw the boundaries. For example, you could say, "This basket is for your stuffed animals. When you have so many stuffed animals that they no longer fit in the basket, you will need to choose a few to give away." Or, "This cupboard is for your games. When you have so many board games that they no longer fit in this cupboard, you will need to donate a few until your games fit." Don't go much larger than a cupboard, though, or the limit will lose its effectiveness. With teens or young adults who are getting ready to go out on their own, set a reasonable number of boxes you are willing to store for them and then ask them to get rid of the rest or move it out with them.

Choose a reasonable number as a limit. Your child can help with this. How many Barbie dolls do you really want? Do you only play with two at a time? Then keep only two. How many baseballs, soccer balls, or basketballs are needed? Keep what you need, and donate the rest. A number limit can be placed on video games, books, dolls, Lego sets, and almost anything you can think of. You can also use a number as a purging goal: "I would like you to choose five books to give away."

Use a date or event as a limit. For example, you might say, "You can keep those decorations in your room until Christmas. After Christmas, they need to come down." Or, "You need to get rid of all the clothes you've outgrown before school starts."

Be the limit enforcer. First, give your children the choice to obey the limit for themselves. However, in some cases, you may need to warn them that if they do not follow the limit by a certain time, you will make the decision for them—and they may not like what you decide! For example, I know one mom who told her son to get rid of three Lego sets. When he was unable to make the decision because it was just too painful, she did it for him. Luckily, she chose wisely, and he was grateful for the help. But if your children want to avoid the pain of a bad choice ("You gave away my favorite Barbie!"), they need to do the hard work of sorting, choosing, and purging themselves. As I like to tell my kids, "If you don't like to take care of your things, I don't either, and then I'll get rid of them so neither of us has to take care of them."

PART TWO

Mind

four

Schedule

How Much Is Too Much?

Beware the barrenness of a busy life.

Socrates

I'll admit it — I have always been one of those people who *likes* to be busy. In fact, the irony of writing a chapter about decluttering my schedule when in many ways my schedule feels more jam-packed than it has ever been has not escaped me. Because for me, most often it's the busier, the better. I'm never more productive than when my to-do list is longer than what I actually have time for. Somehow the challenge of having too much to do always seems to motivate me to work a little harder and be a little more efficient. The only time I procrastinate is when I've got only a few things to do — then somehow I can't seem to get anything done. My margin, my "white space," happens between the hours of 9:00 p.m. and 5:00 a.m., when I am sleeping. Otherwise I am always in motion, always thinking about the next item on my list.

And I'm not ashamed to say — I kind of like it that way.

Except, of course, when I don't like it. When all these commitments and obligations and expectations get to be just a little too much, and suddenly I feel like I'm drowning, like I'm always behind and will never catch up. I start waking up earlier and going to bed later, just to squeeze a little more productivity out of the day, but that only ends up leaving me sleep deprived. Inevitably the lack of sleep catches up to me and I get sick, which only gets me falling farther and farther behind.

Yes, I like to be busy. Except when I don't.

My husband, Chuck, not surprisingly, is once again my polar opposite. He hates to be busy and can't stand having a whole list of things to do hanging over his head. In the face of an overwhelming to-do list, he tends to freeze, not knowing where to begin. He is paralyzed by the weight of everything that needs to be done. He requires a lot more margin in his daily life, blank space to just be, to sit and savor a cup of coffee, to read the news reports, or to watch the girls do cartwheels on the lawn. He needs time to be still, to take a nap, to just do *nothing*.

And he's not afraid to say he likes it *that* way.

My frantic pace drives him insane.

It has taken us nearly ten years of marriage to come to grips with the fact that when it comes to the question of *how much is too much*, our answers look very different. In fact, I think we're still coming to grips with that fact. Because as much as I crave activity and projects and purpose, Chuck craves rest and calm and meaningful moments. Where I want a plan of attack, he wants room for spontaneity.

Finding a middle ground has been—and continues to be—a work in progress, but our starting point has simply been to recognize the fact that our comfort zones fall in very different places. What feels just right to me feels chaotic to him, and what feels absolutely perfect to him feels painfully slow to me—and neither one of us can say we are completely right or completely wrong. But as a family, our schedule has to reflect both our personalities, as well as the personalities of our kids, or we will end up driving ourselves—and each other—completely crazy. I need enough action to feel productive, while he needs enough margin to feel recharged. And our kids need enough activities to keep them stimulated but enough downtime to keep them relaxed and happy.

Which brings us right back to the question, *How much is too much?*

HOW MUCH IS TOO MUCH?

Not sure whether you've crossed the line from productive to overcommitted? Use this list to identify any red flags that may be happening in your life. For added accountability, go through this list with your spouse or a close friend. They may see signs you are not aware of. If the answer to more than three of the following questions is yes, then it might be time to make some serious changes in your schedule.*

Physical Symptoms

- Are you or other members of your family frequently sick?
- Do you often feel tired or run-down?
- Do you or other members of your family get frequent headaches or migraines?
- Do you or other members of your family have unexplained stomach pains or digestive issues?
- Do you or other members of your family have frequent injuries from sports or excessive exercise?

Emotional Symptoms

- Do you often feel overwhelmed, like things are spinning out of control?
- Do you often feel scattered, confused, or forgetful?
- Do you often feel stressed or anxious?
- Do you ever feel angry for no reason?
- Do you ever feel sad, depressed, or like you just can't cope?

*For instructions on how to access this quiz online, see page 219 at the back of the book.

Relational Symptoms

- Do you and your spouse fight frequently?
- Do you frequently get frustrated with your kids for doing normal kid things?
- Do you rarely see your close friends or extended family?
- Do your feelings get hurt easily?
- Do you feel like you never have time to spend with the people you love?

Spiritual Symptoms

- Do you ever neglect prayer and Bible reading because you just don't have time?
- Do you regularly skip church because other activities take precedence?
- Have you developed any destructive behaviors, such as drinking, doing drugs, or overspending to cope with the stress of trying to keep up?
- Do you feel like God is very far away?
- Do you struggle with a nagging sense of guilt?

Practical Symptoms

- Have you recently missed appointments or important dates because you just couldn't keep up?
- Are you ever late paying your bills?
- Have you dropped the ball or made any mistakes at work?
- Is your home frequently messy because there is no time to clean?

- Do you spend more money than you should on convenience food and eating out because there isn't time to cook or plan meals?
- Is your budget out of control?
- Do you feel like you are constantly running from one thing to the next?
- Are your kids struggling in school?

Combating the Culture of Busy

We all know that family. Yours might even *be* that family — the ones constantly running from one activity to the next, from work to school, from sporting event to play practice, from dance class to piano lesson, from PTA meeting to Cub Scouts, from Bible study to book club. The family that considers sitting down to dinner together as a time when you're all eating fast food from McDonald's drive-through in the car on the way to yet another *thing*. The family whose main communication during the week consists of logistics — who's picking up who when, and what time you need to be where. The family whose life has become just one big series of events, appointments, and obligations. The family whose evenings are spent rushing from here to there, then rushing home to finish homework, go to bed, and start all over again the next day. The family that simply doesn't have time to slow down.

It's a frenzied pace, one fueled by a culture that not only embraces this sort of go-go-go mentality but perpetuates it. The underlying message is that if our lives aren't completely full, they don't count. And it's not just *our* lives; it's our kids' lives as well. Whereas kids used to have the freedom to just be kids — to run around outside, ride bikes, play, and use their imagination — they now have structured activities filling up nearly every minute of their days. Between more homework and more sports, more clubs and lessons and classes and groups, kids have almost zero time to just be *kids*.

The problem with such jam-packed schedules is not that it is unmanageable, at least some of the time, or even that the activities filling up every time slot aren't worthwhile — many times they are. No, the main problem is that this culture of busy, this idea that we can't slow down, can't stop running from one thing to the next for fear that we might miss out, or worse, that our kids might fall behind, becomes a constant presence in our lives — the most important presence in our lives. Without really intending it to happen, the busyness becomes our first priority, the thing we value above all else.

The busyness becomes our idol.

We can't slow down for fear that our lives won't matter if we do. The busyness gives us purpose; the jam-packed schedule provides meaning to otherwise empty lives. But here's the truth: A busy life is not the same as a meaningful one. Athletic, successful, or talented children do not make us more important. Activities, obligations, and commitments do not make us count. If we're looking for the answer to our frustration, despair, and hopelessness in a full calendar, *we will never find it there*. In fact, quite often, the fuller our calendars become, the emptier our hearts feel.

The reality is that most of the time, even when we think we might be doing okay, we're still failing, still messing up, still dropping the ball and forgetting to keep our priorities straight. And while that may sound a little depressing, I tend to think that the fact that each and every one of us has failed is actually quite liberating, and this is why: Only when we realize how desperately we need grace are we able to accept it — and to give it back to ourselves and to others.

In Matthew 11:28, Jesus says, "Come to me, all you who are weary and burdened, and I will give you rest. Take my yoke upon you and learn from me, for I am gentle and humble in heart, and you will find rest for your souls. For my yoke is easy and my burden is light."

So often in our lives, we find ourselves striving for a grace we have already been given. We fill our days with activity, running from one thing to the next, hoping to gain meaning and purpose, but never quite finding it. The world tells us we have to *do* something to matter, but the reality is the opposite. It's already been done. The most important task on our to-do list is to simply accept it.

The Choices We Make

My daughter Maggie recently finished the third grade, which is evidently the year when the homework really starts to roll in. On a daily basis, she was normally assigned worksheets for both math and vocabulary, as well as twenty to thirty minutes of required reading. As part of her school's intensive music program, she also had to practice the violin for at least twenty minutes, and then, if she had time, she was encouraged to spend time on the online learning programs IXL .com and MobyMax.com. It all added up to about an hour and a half of work each afternoon, and that's if she was actually being efficient with her time. In my biased parental opinion, it was a lot — too much for an eight-year-old kid who was already going to school from 8:00 a.m. to 3:30 p.m. every day. Call me old-fashioned, but I still believe kids need time just to be kids.

This created an interesting dilemma for my husband and me: Should we enforce the stringent homework requirements, or should we ignore them? Ultimately, we decided to take our concerns directly to Maggie's teacher, whom we greatly respected, and she assured us that it was perfectly okay to skip homework sometimes. Thus, we decided we would leave the choice up to Maggie. While we stood firm on the violin requirement, we told her she was free to choose whether or not to do the rest of the work. If she wanted to do the work and be rewarded at school the next day, she could, but if she just wanted to play with her sister, that was okay too.

Maggie, our consummate firstborn overachieving perfectionist, adored her teacher and wanted nothing more than to please her. She was highly motivated by the thought of earning straws, as five straws earned a prize from the treasure box. While many kids would have welcomed the excuse to do nothing, she almost always chose to do her work.

One night, however, while Maggie had been practicing her violin, I asked her younger sister Annie to play a game with me. Annie chose Skip-Bo, a family favorite. Maggie, who was just finishing up her violin practice, asked if she could play too. I explained to Maggie that while she was welcome to play with us, if she chose to play, she'd have no time to finish her homework. She agreed and sat down at the table for a rousing, extremely close game, which Maggie won by one card. But then we said it was time for bed, and instead of reveling in her narrow victory, Maggie burst into tears.

"I have to finish my homework," she wailed, "or I won't get any straws!"

"I'm sorry, honey," I said, looking down at her panic-stricken face, "but you knew this was the deal. If you chose to play, there wouldn't be time to finish your homework. Now it's time for bed, because you are a growing girl and you need lots of sleep. Remember, sweetie, actions have consequences. Sometimes when you choose one thing, it means you are saying no to something else. And that's just the way it is."

At my daughter's eight years of age, this idea of actions having consequences was a tough pill for her to swallow. But I have to admit this is often a tough pill for *me* to swallow as well. You see, I want to say yes to everything too. I want to say yes to my kids, who are vying for my time and attention and who need their mom. I want to say yes to my husband, who for the most part is pretty patient and long-suffering but who needs to know he is more important than everything else I have going on. I want to say yes to volunteering at my kids' school, to being the cochair of the PTA, to writing a guest article for another website, to working with Compassion International, to helping out a fellow blogger who needs advice, to speaking at a conference, to growing a vegetable garden and starting a compost pile, to meeting with people who may have an amazing business opportunity, to being a good sister, a good daughter, a good boss, a good friend.

I want to say yes to everything, but when I do, I end up failing at many of them. My kids are disappointed because I am distracted. My husband is irritated because I never have enough time to just sit and talk. My writing suffers because it was rushed. I am constantly sick from too much travel and too little sleep. My garden dies. My friends get ignored. I drop the ball on the fund-raiser I had promised to lead. I completely forget to attend the last PTA meeting of the year — the very one I had told everyone else was so important.

Actions have consequences. Sometimes when we choose one thing, it means we are saying no to something else. When we choose to say yes to every opportunity, every obligation, we inevitably say no to other things — things that should matter more. Like our families and our faith. Like our sleep and our health. Like our patience and our sanity.

The problem is not that we are saying yes to bad things. They are all good things. Amazing things. We want to be the moms who volunteer at school. We want to be the person others can come to for advice. We want to do what we can to use the gifts God has given us to make a difference in the world. We want to pursue our interests and hobbies and goals and dreams. We want to be everything to everyone.

We want to say yes to everything. But what we really need to learn is how to say no. Actions have consequences. If we don't carefully choose our own NOs, they will invariably be chosen for us. And that is something none of us can afford.

Learning to Say No

No. Why is it that one of the most common words in the English language is so difficult to say? I can't speak for anyone else, but for me, there are lots of reasons I have a hard time with that one simple word. I get caught off guard. I want to please people. I don't want to be mean or unhelpful. I don't want to burn a bridge or miss an opportunity or miss out on something fun. I don't want people to be mad or upset with me or to speak poorly of me. And so, time and time again, I say yes when I shouldn't. *Often at the expense of something else.*

I forget that saying yes too many times makes me feel overwhelmed and stressed-out. It causes me to neglect the rest of the things in my life that I really *should* be doing and *could* be doing if I had just said no. Even worse, it makes me resentful of the asker and makes me feel underappreciated and overcommitted.

I don't think I'm alone.

In fact, Lysa TerKeurst recently wrote a great book on this very subject called *The Best Yes.* In anticipation of its release, she wrote in her blog, "We have to slow the rhythm of rush in our lives so the best of who we are can emerge."[4]

Easier said than done, right?

In my own life, I have found that I have to stay very conscious of what happens when I *don't* say no, and even then, it is hard. But I am learning, slowly, that in order to become *good* at saying no, I have to arm myself with a handful of tools that will help me say no without feeling bad and without upsetting the person doing the asking. They are certainly not foolproof, and I certainly haven't mastered them yet, but these five guidelines might just help you too.

1. Start and end with a positive. Soften the blow of saying no by including a few positive statements before and after the word *no.* These positive phrases can help take the focus off the negative and act like a cushion to the one word we have such a hard time using. Instead of being the big fat meanie we fear we will be perceived as, we become the person who sees value in the other party and what they are asking us to do.

Here's how it works. Begin with a compliment: "That sounds wonderful!" Or, "What a great idea!"

Gently say no: "I'd absolutely love to do this, but I can't right now."

Finish with a positive: "I'm so honored you would ask. I know it will be great!"

Sometimes we get so caught up in not wanting to disappoint someone that we forget how powerful an effective delivery can be in any situation, but especially when we are giving bad news. Being prepared and positive (but firm) can greatly increase the chances of our audience reacting positively as well.

2. Don't answer right away. Before answering a request, let the asker know you will get back to them. Make a habit of taking a breather, no matter the request, so you have a moment to think about how you really want to answer. It is perfectly okay to say, "I will have to check my schedule," or, "I have to think about it," or, "I need to talk with my spouse" before giving a final answer.

Many times we say yes because we feel obligated to accept while in person or because we are so caught up in the excitement of the opportunity or the need to please that we forget how little time we have. Taking a moment and getting back to the person later will give you time to think and respond appropriately without committing yourself to something you don't want to do. In addition, by taking the time to consider the request, you are indicating to the asker that you are thoughtful and considerate of their needs (and perhaps nudging them to treat you with the same thoughtful consideration!).

Waiting to give an answer is probably the easiest way to begin your journey to effectively using the word *no*. For me, particularly in the blogging and business world, it is the response I most commonly use. Pausing before answering allows me to gain a moment of clarity, to bounce the request off a few people to get their thoughts and opinions about the situation, and sometimes even to find someone else who is interested. Everybody wins!

3. Change the channel. When the asker is very assertive, aggressive, or good at making you feel guilty, it can be very hard to say no in person. In these cases, try changing the channel. Ask for time to give a response and then respond to an in-person or phone request through a nonconfrontational channel of communication, such as an email or a text message. Having a firm no in writing without having a verbal conversation helps you avoid the trap of back-and-forth convincing, especially when the person who is doing the asking is much more forceful or persuasive than you are. It is also much easier to type *no* than say it!

4. Refer a friend. When you are asked to do something you are not interested in doing or don't have enough time to do, it can be much easier to say no by referring someone else who might do the job even better. Most of us know at least one or two people who like to say yes to everything or who love being involved or who are looking to plug in somewhere else. Perhaps it is someone who recently moved to the area and hasn't found their tribe just yet or another person who happens to be an expert in this area and would gladly take this task on and do an even better job.

By providing a name of someone else who may be interested, you can go from being the person who says no to the person who helped. There's a big difference between the two, and the latter is one both parties can feel great about. Instead of obligating yourself, drop a name and walk away feeling helpful.

5. Let someone else do the dirty work. If you are really struggling with saying no and setting limits, it is entirely appropriate and helpful to enlist the help of others — perhaps a spouse, a close friend, a coworker, or a sister — to advocate on your behalf. Is it cheating to not do it yourself? Maybe, but not always. A mediator can say no for you, explaining that while you really want to say yes, right now there is just no way you can make it work. A friend or spouse might be able to convey just how bad you feel, with fewer hurt feelings on either end.

Alternatively, you can refer to your spouse's or family's opinions or needs as a reminder to the asker (and yourself) that you have other commitments and people you need to honor. "My husband likes us to spend Sunday as a family day," you might say. Or, "I can't take anything on during Little League season; it's just too crazy."

In the end, a simple, direct *no* is usually the most effective. It eliminates the expectation of any other possible outcome and quickly frees up both the person asking and the person answering. It allows you to check off the item on your mental list instead of wasting additional thought on it. Even the Bible advocates a direct approach. Jesus, in Matthew 5:37, says, "All you need to say is simply 'Yes' or 'No'; anything beyond this comes from the evil one."

In other words, be quick. Be considerate. Be confident. But say no.

Discovering Balance

When I was a little girl growing up in a conservative, religious, Dutch immigrant community, the concept of Sunday rest was taken very seriously. We went to church, usually twice, but did very little else. Stores were closed, and everyone stayed home. After coffee and a light lunch, sometimes we napped or played games or spent time together as a family, but our chores and yard work were all done on Saturday, because Sunday was a day of rest.

I actually hadn't even thought about this for years, until I read an article recently in the *Wall Street Journal*, detailing how this same philosophy is still very much adhered to in Germany. Shopping centers and retail stores are closed, and noise ordinances prohibit residents from mowing their lawns, working on construction projects, or even recycling glass bottles or driving heavy trucks on the road. Countrywide, Sunday is set aside as a day to refresh and recharge.[5] And I think it's more than a coincidence that Germany — in spite of its day of rest and probably even *because* of it — is considered the most productive country in the European Union. With their Sunday rest and their legendary six-week-long vacations, along with their powerhouse productivity, Germans seem to have achieved that elusive thing called "balance."

Balance is one of those words we throw around a lot, often perceiving it as a higher state of being that we are all constantly striving for, hoping for, and trying to find. We might not know exactly what it looks like, but we know we don't have it. And so we keep trying.

But what is balance? What exactly does that word mean?

Does it mean a life carefully segmented into different categories, each of which is filled with an equal amount of time and energy, lined up in our minds like a row of clear canisters, each one filled with the same number of marbles? We've got our family canister, our work canister, our church canister, our friends canister, our volunteer canister, our fun canister, our rest canister — and as long as we can keep them all filled at the same level, we are maintaining balance.

Is it a pie chart, a circle of ourselves segmented into all the different aspects of our life? The more equal the slices, the more balance we've achieved?

Is it a tightrope? A thin line we are constantly walking across, trying not to fall into the pit of catastrophe below? A single wire holding us above the brink of utter chaos?

Is it a scale? A delicate balancing act between work and family or between obligations and relaxation, between the things we *have* to do and the things we *want* to do?

What is balance?

Honestly, I don't think it is necessarily *any* of those things, though sometimes it feels like all of them. The problem with striving for balance in a DIY culture that is constantly reminding us to do more, have more, and be more is that we think achieving balance is something we can DO. Instead, I think balance happens in the margin. Balance doesn't happen from the things we are doing; it is what happens when we *stop* doing. Learning to say no is the first step to a more balanced life. Remembering to rest is the second. And guess what? There is no third step.

Balance comes from rest.

We can't create balance in our life. We can't discover it or make room for it or split our time equally and hope we find it or make sure our pie slices are equal or simply keep walking that tightrope a little bit longer. There is nothing we can *do*.

Balance comes from rest.

As much as I'd like to take credit for this epiphany, it doesn't come from me (or even from the Germans). On the contrary, it has been with us from the very beginning: "By the seventh day God had finished the work he had been doing; so on the seventh day he rested from all his work. Then God blessed the seventh day and made it holy, because on it he rested from all the work of creating that he had done" (Genesis 2:2–3).

And then, in Exodus, on top of Mount Sinai, God reminded the Israelites again: "Six days you shall labor and do all your work, but the seventh day is a sabbath to the LORD your God ... For in six days the LORD made the heavens and the earth, the sea, and all that is in them, but he rested on the seventh day. Therefore the LORD blessed the Sabbath day and made it holy" (20:9–11).

We were made to rest.

I will readily admit this is a tough pill for me to swallow. As a mom who has worked very hard to build my own business, I have a very hard time turning it off. It doesn't help that the bulk of my work happens online, reaching readers all around the world. There is no time, day or night, seven days a week, 365 days a year, that someone isn't wanting something from me or that there isn't something I could be doing. I like to be productive. I want to do my best. Not only that, but my family depends on my income. As a responsible adult, I feel a self-imposed pressure to succeed that never goes away.

But we were made to rest.

I was made to rest.

So while finding balance isn't something I can *do*, giving myself and my family time for rest is something I can be more intentional about. Here are some concrete ways to establish more rest in your home:

1. **Take one day off per week.** Consciously and purposefully set aside one day per week that is solely for rest and relaxation. Block it out in your schedule, and don't be afraid to make your day off known to friends, family members, and coworkers. After all, if you don't respect your day off, no one else will either.

2. **Unplug.** Set aside screen-free time in your day to allow yourself time away from the constant stream of connectivity. Turn off your cell phone, shut down the computer, unplug the TV. Encourage the other members of your family to do the same.

3. **Take a nap.** Research has shown again and again the effectiveness of taking a short power nap during the day. A short nap can recharge your brain and make you more productive. It can also improve your memory, boost your creativity, and even help reduce stress.

4. **Spend time outside.** There is something almost magical about getting outside in the fresh air, even if just for a few minutes. And the benefits aren't just in our heads — spending time outside on a regular basis is good for the immune system, makes us feel more relaxed, gives us more energy, and helps reduce stress.

5. **Discover what relaxes you, and do it.** For different people, this will mean different things. My husband loves to just sit and enjoy doing nothing. I actually feel more tense when I'm just sitting around, but I love playing card games, reading, or spending time in my garden. Don't feel like you need to adopt someone else's idea of relaxation, but do figure out what works for you — and then do it.

The key to resting—and I mean *really* resting—is actually allowing your mind and body to take a break even when there is more to do. Because there will always be more to do. Every day. For the rest of our lives. Look at it this way—if God could take a day off without the world falling apart, so can we.

Busyness isn't necessarily bad, all on its own. It's great to have things we enjoy doing, to have hobbies and interests, and to be productive. We were made to work. That said, an overbooked schedule can easily become destructive if we let it become the most important thing in our lives, the thing that gives us meaning and purpose. The only solution, then, is to combat this culture of busy with grace, to realize that our choices have consequences, to learn how to say no, and to discover balance by giving ourselves plenty of space for rest.

HOW TO CREATE A SCHEDULE THAT WORKS FOR YOUR FAMILY

Developing a schedule and routine that works for all the different needs of you and your family can sometimes feel like a daunting task. How can you possibly fit it all in? Sometimes the only answer is to take a step back and look at the bigger picture—what things are nonnegotiable, what things are only optional, and what things you would secretly like to get out of. The following exercise is one that should be completed with your spouse, as well as with your kids if they are old enough to participate.

To do this exercise, you will need a blank sheet of paper, a blank weekly calendar, and a different color pen for each member of the family.*

---

*For instructions on how to download a free template of a weekly calendar, see page 219 at the back of the book.

STEP 1
Determine Your Nonnegotiables

What are the activities you absolutely must do? This includes things like work and school but also the things you are absolutely not willing to compromise on or skip, such as going to church, eating dinner as a family at least three times a week, or reserving one day a week for rest. (Hint: If your day of rest is not a nonnegotiable, it should be!) Write them all down on your blank sheet of paper, including the times they take place, and then block out the times on your calendar, using the different colored pens for different family members.

STEP 2
Determine Your Optionals

Now make a list of all the other activities your family takes part in. This can include everything from sporting events or music lessons to clubs, associations, and youth groups. It may also include social events, Bible studies or book clubs, and volunteer opportunities. Try to write down as many things as possible that take up your time on a regular basis. Now rank them in order of importance, from the things you love and want to do, to the things you don't really enjoy or want to be spending time on. (If it makes more sense, you can do separate rankings for each family member.) No ties are allowed—this will force you to determine which activities really matter most to each of you. Rewrite the list in order of importance.

STEP 3
Eliminate the Unessential

Once you've established a hierarchy for the activities in your life, it is time to begin reevaluating your priorities and the way you are spending your time. Starting from the bottom with the activities that are least important or enjoyable for you, decide together as a family if it might be feasible to cut them out. How much time could you free up in your week by eliminating a few of the activities you are least excited about? What could you do instead? What might the consequences be of saying no? Is it worth it? Cross out as many items as you can.

STEP 4
Fill in the Gaps

Add the remaining activities to your schedule, using different colored pens for each family member. Are there conflicts in the schedule? Can they be resolved or worked around? If not, give priority to the nonnegotiables first and then to whichever activity is higher up on the list. Let the hierarchy be your guideline for deciding what to do.

All in all, it is a pretty simple but amazingly effective system because it forces your family to make clear choices about what is most important. And in the end, having clarity about what matters most is the only solution to creating a schedule that really works.

five

Paperwork

Drowning in a Sea of Information

Clutter is the physical manifestation of unmade decisions fueled by procrastination.

Christina Scalise

A part of me has always hated paperwork and the tediousness of trying to be a responsible adult, one who pays bills on time and balances the checkbook on a regular basis. As a single girl in my twenties, I had very little paperwork — I didn't have investments to keep track of, and the only bills I really had to worry about paying each month were my rent and car payments. After I got married, things became much more complicated. My husband, nineteen years my senior, had already been a responsible adult for quite some time. He had investments, retirement plans, IRAs, and 401(k) plans to keep track of, a little here and a little there, frustratingly scattered in a hodgepodge of accounts across the country, dotting the map as a testament to all the different cities where he had worked. Hurricane Charley only added to our confusion. Suddenly, on top of everything else, we were dealing with a catastrophic insurance claim and acting as our own contractor, which meant meticulously keeping track of every loss, every bit of damage, and every single repair. Then, right around that same time, the era of digital data descended en masse. Suddenly the pile of mail on the counter was nothing compared to the hundreds of emails flooding my inbox. The need to respond was endless.

Even so, I never totally understood the feeling of drowning in a sea of information and paperwork until I had children. From the moment my oldest daughter was born, there were not just the added responsibilities of securing a Social Security card and birth certificate in order to legitimize this brand-new human in my arms, but the need to prepare for her future, to keep track of her medical records and immunization chart, and to fully document every single moment of her childhood with photos, journal keeping, and an artfully arranged baby book. It's enough to induce a panic attack just thinking about it.

But babies were the easy part, because school has brought this crisis of paperwork to a whole new, completely terrifying level. From spelling tests to art projects, birthday invitations to math homework, the steady flow of paper never really ends. And then there's the thing that nightmares are made of—the dreaded Thursday Folder. Every week, without fail, my kids come home with what appears to be an innocent green folder but which is, in fact, the source of more stress than even seems possible. In this folder, we find paper after paper, each one demanding our attention, calling us to act, compelling us to remember yet one more thing. Whether it is a permission slip for a field trip, a reminder of the PTA meeting happening next week, a guilt-inducing reminder of the need for baskets for the next fundraiser, the monthly lunch menu that needs to be returned, the book order that needs to be placed, the application that needs to be filled out, the class party that needs to be planned, the program that needs to be remembered, there is always One. More. Thing.

Inevitably, this combination of tests, worksheets, coloring pages, art projects, permission slips, event flyers, menus, applications, birthday invitations, and reminders ends up in an ever-increasing pile on the counter, one that eventually becomes too overwhelming to even deal with and too chaotic to find anything, which means that the all-important events we were determined not to miss this time get buried and forgotten until it's too late.

At our first PTA meeting last year, I jokingly suggested that as a fund-raiser, we let parents bid on the option to never get another piece of paper sent home from school. Just think of it, I said, how many parents would give anything to have the option to just be free of that ever-growing, never-ending, completely overwhelming stack that crowds their kitchen counter. The rest of the group laughed, and we moved on to our real plans, but the truth is that I was only half joking. I really would pay to never have to see another piece of paper sent home from my kids' school, and I'm guessing I'm not the only one.

But as much as I'd like to blame my current paper problem on the Thursday Folder, the reality is that this sea of information I'm drowning in isn't caused by any *one* thing. Yes, the world I live in has bombarded me with noise, expectations, and things to remember, and with bills to pay, cards to write, photographs to organize, statements to file, permission slips to sign, emails to respond to, and so on and so on. But that doesn't mean I'm not culpable or that I don't bear the responsibility for how I react to this noise. If I'm really being honest with myself, I know that most of the time my paper problem is really a procrastination problem. It's not the paperwork that is stressing me out; it is the obligation that gets attached to it, and my unwillingness to deal with it.

My friend Glynnis Whitwer recently wrote a book called *Taming the To-Do List* about tackling this procrastination issue that so many of us struggle with. In it, she describes the shift of responsibility that has happened as a result of technology. She writes, "It used to be that the burden to communicate was on the one with the need or the question. My, how times have changed. With the advent of technology ... the burden to communicate has shifted ... Now you email me and it's my job to respond. You text me, and I better text back."[6]

The problem with this shift is that we spend our days reacting to other people's demands and expectations rather than proactively figuring out what needs to be done (and then doing it). The resulting pile of paperwork and overflowing inbox is our resistance to these demands. And the pile of paperwork on our counter becomes the visual representation of that internal battle between what we want to do and what others tell us we should do.

So what's the solution?

How do we reconcile this need to tame the raging sea of information overload with our own internal struggle to not spend the bulk of our days reacting to everyone else's needs? Is it even possible to do both? Is the answer to finally gaining full control over our paperwork really just a life of total self-sacrifice, of giving up our own hopes and dreams and interests in the interest of keeping everyone else happy?

I don't think so.

In fact, I would argue that this approach can ultimately lead to even more frustration, which will in turn lead to *more* procrastination and an even bigger problem. No, the only solution is to develop some sort of internal filter, one that allows us to quickly, easily, and instantly determine what is important — what we actually need to deal with — and what can wait or be forgotten altogether. Once we've filtered the influx, it becomes a little easier to act immediately on the important stuff and to leave the rest behind.

Developing an Information Filter

My mother-in-law, Marie, was meticulous about keeping records. In fact, she was *obsessed* with them. After she died, we discovered drawer upon drawer and cabinet after cabinet *filled* with the papers she had kept. She had kept every bank statement since 1940, every single canceled check, every utility bill she had ever paid, every credit card statement, every insurance statement, every tax bill, every deed, and every title, even for houses and cars she no longer owned. In her sixty-plus years, I doubt very much that she ever looked at any of them or that there was ever a need to go back through them, and yet, there it was—an entire lifetime of useless paper.

While it might be easy to shrug off this compulsion to save everything as the cringeworthy but ultimately harmless neurosis of a sweet old lady, a woman who grew up during the Depression, a woman who was determined to do better for her children than her own mother did for her, I often wonder how much happier she could have been if she had just let all that paper stuff go.

You see, Marie was a wonderful woman with a huge heart, someone I loved dearly and miss to this day. But she was also a woman consumed by worry, haunted by the paperwork and records she had worked so hard to keep her entire life. She lived in Florida with my husband and me for the last few years of her life, but when we returned to her house in Chicago after she died, we found hundreds of handwritten notes and instructions for what to do after she died, written over and over and over again, scattered all over the house— tucked into books, taped to the walls. We realized she had spent the bulk of her final years in her house sitting there alone, thinking only about what would happen to all these records upon her death. Her obsession with the papers she had kept and her constant concern for keeping it all in order prevented her from actually enjoying her golden years in peace.

And while it is easy to feel a whole lot of sadness for Marie and for all that time she wasted worrying about the endless piles of papers that were ultimately bound for the dumpster, I find I am often guilty of the same habits. I just haven't yet accumulated sixty-plus years of it. If anything, I'm *worse* off than she was.

We all are.

Just consider the statistics. Ninety percent of the current data in the world was generated in the *last two years*.[7] The amount of information available to us since the dawn of the Internet age has literally exploded. In fact, according to Google CEO Eric Schmidt, the amount of information is increasing so quickly that in our current culture, the world creates more information every *two* days than was created from the beginning of time through 2003.[8]

Yikes.

Without a way of dealing with this overload of information now, it is not only possible that we are destined to live out a life of continual stress and worry; it is practically inevitable. The only way to avoid being washed away by this tsunami of incoming data and to avoid drowning in this sea of relentless information is to equip ourselves with a battle plan. We need a failproof strategy. We need to develop an information filter for our lives.

So what is this information filter? How does it work, and how do we develop it? Basically, an information filter is a set of internal rules that tells our brain what to pay attention to and what to ignore. It is a guideline we establish for dealing with the enormously overwhelming amount of data being thrown at us at any given time. If used properly, our information filter automatically sifts through the noise to bring us what is relevant and to help us focus on the things that matter most while disregarding the rest.

At my company, Living Well Spending Less, Inc., we receive hundreds of emails every single day. I could easily spend my entire day doing nothing but responding and reacting to the myriad of data requests, press inquiries, reader questions, and action items that come in. In fact, I could spend my whole day responding to email and still never get to it all. However, if I spent my whole day attending to email, I wouldn't have any time to write blog posts or books, travel and speak, teach my blogging course, manage all the other aspects of my business, or even to spend quality time with my family. As such, my team and I have had to develop some pretty strict guidelines for how we deal with email. My assistant, Natalie, has a list of email rules — essentially "if this, then that" responses — that she uses to easily filter the hundreds of emails down to a very manageable handful. While she used to have to keep the list of rules close at hand every time she opened our inbox, eventually the rules and guidelines became so familiar, so automatic, that most of the time, she doesn't even have to think about them.

That is exactly how an information filter should work in our personal lives. While it does take time and energy to create a set of hard-and-fast rules for ourselves, and while it also takes a certain amount of discipline to start adhering to those rules, eventually they become automatic and practically effortless. The filter we create to sift through the information makes the decision for us, thereby allowing us to stop procrastinating. Instead of letting the paperwork pile up on our counters and hang over our heads, we simply deal with it and move on.

And of course, while all of this sounds well and good in theory, in practice it might be a little overwhelming to even know where to begin when it comes to setting up these rules for dealing with the information overload in your life and for creating the filter that will help you navigate this tidal wave of data and paperwork without feeling like you are drowning in the process. These simple steps might help you along the way:

1. **Identify the problem.** Where is the bulk of your paper and data stress coming from? Is it the bills piled up on your counter? The stack of yet-to-be filed paperwork on your desk that you don't quite know what to do with but are afraid to throw away? The mountain of thank-you cards you feel obligated to write? The 2,367 unread emails in your inbox? The ten thousand-plus pictures you have taken since getting your first digital camera in 2005? The piles of unread magazines or newspapers?

2. **Determine your priorities.** Who and what is most important to you? Is it making sure your bills are paid on time? Is it finally getting your photographs in order? Is it keeping track of your most important paperwork, such as passports, birth certificates, and social security cards? Is it being able to find the document or project you are currently working on? Is it staying up-to-date with your friends and family? What do you care about most?

3. **Create solutions.** Based on both the problems and priorities you've identified, where is your most critical need for a solution? Start there. Thus, if your biggest paper problem is the mail piling up on your counter, and your biggest priority is figuring out how to pay your bills on time, then the first solution you will need to work on is determining what to do with all that mail, as well as figuring out exactly when your bills need to be paid so you pay them on time.

4. **Establish firm guidelines.** This is where the rule comes in — the "if this, then that." Once you've established both the problem (the "if this") and the solution (the "then that"), setting up the filter is easy. But don't stop at just thinking about it — take the time to write it down. Writing stuff down makes it real, and once it is real, you can't ignore it.

5. **Stick with it.** This is both the hard and the easy part. Once you've created your filter, you need to apply it again and again until it becomes automatic, a habit you just can't help but do. This takes time. So resolve to stick with it and not quit, no matter what.

Creating Solutions That Work for Everyone

Our problem with paperwork and information overload often boils down to an inability to simply make a decision. We become overwhelmed by the demand to continually react to the endless stream of requests, needs, obligations, action items, and information being hurled at us daily. The simplest solution, then, is a filter to help us sift through this influx, stop procrastinating, and quickly and easily make decisions. Even so, these decisions require a practical solution to make them work. After all, if the rules you are establishing say "if this, then that," your "that" needs to be a concrete solution to whatever the "this" may be.

For example, one of my paper problems is the approximately seven thousand worksheets, tests, and assignments that get sent home from school with my older daughter Maggie nearly every single day. Through trial and error (and a few low moments in my mothering career), I have discovered that Maggie gets really upset if I throw away her hard work, at least right away. She wants me to save it. However, I have also discovered that she doesn't mind throwing things away at the end of a school year, when we can go through the whole pile and pick out just a few highlights to save and then toss the rest. Our solution is a bin at the top of her closet that collects all of her papers for the entire year. When she comes home from school each day with a new stack of papers to show me, I immediately look through them, praise her for a job well done, and place all the papers in the bin. Our "this" is the school papers, while our "that" is the bin at the top of her closet. Simple, easy, and effective. However, without creating the solution—the bin— my "that" could just as easily end up being "stacking the pile of papers on the counter" or "throwing them away," the first of which would drive me crazy and the second of which would hurt Maggie's feelings.

If you live by yourself, it is relatively easy to create solutions that will work because you are the only one who has to adhere to them. There are no other feelings to think about and no other organizational styles to contend with. This does not necessarily mean it is easy—everyone's challenges are unique—but as a general rule, the more people you add to the mix, the more opportunity there is for an organizational system to break down. Thus, simple solutions are always the best.

I think sometimes, when it comes to paperwork and digital data, we try to overcomplicate our solutions, creating systems that are confusing and difficult to implement or that don't make sense to anyone but the person who has set them up. So here's my advice—the easier and more intuitive the solution, the more likely every member of your family, from the largest to the smallest, is to follow it. Don't require filing when a simple bin will do. Don't keep what could just as easily be thrown away. Don't create too many folders or steps to follow. Don't insist on perfection.

If you are around my age or older, you may remember this, but in the mid-1990s, a new trend called scrapbooking hit suburbia and became incredibly popular. Scrapbook stores cropped up all over the country, while moms everywhere rushed to host scrapbooking parties. Countless hours were spent crafting beautiful, elaborate pages for these scrapbooks. Every event was represented by die cut letters, embellishments, and an endless array of colorfully printed paper. And while these fancy scrapbooks were certainly creative and often very beautiful, they were also incredibly time-consuming to create. Of all the moms I knew who took up this hobby, every single one of them soon fell hopelessly behind in their efforts. New pictures, new events, and new children were happening far faster than they could document them. The harder they tried to keep up, the more they fell behind. Most of them eventually gave up, especially when digital photos and digital photo books made the process so much easier.

While I don't really have a problem with scrapbooking, especially for anyone who truly enjoys the process as a creative outlet, my point is that scrapbooking — or any other endeavor that can be incredibly complicated and time-consuming — is not a very effective solution for paper and information problems. Simple works; complicated does not.

When it comes to creating simple solutions for your paper problems, it helps to first identify what the problem is and where it is coming from, as well as to your current solution. Thus, if one of your paper problems is the pile of unopened mail that has taken over your kitchen counter, the simplest solution may be a pretty wooden box on that same counter for collecting bills, paired with a nearby recycle bin and a policy of instantly discarding all junk mail and paying bills on the first and fifteenth of the month. Your "this" is your incoming mail; your "that" is the box, recycle bin, and regular schedule for bill paying. Simple. Easy. Effective. Done.

SIMPLE PAPER STORAGE SOLUTIONS

When it comes to discovering the perfect system of organization, the truth is that everyone's brains work a little bit differently. Some people like piles, while others can't stand piles anywhere. You will have to work to figure out what system works best for your brain; just keep in mind that the simpler the system, the more likely you are to use it. The following paper storage solutions are the ones I have found to work best for me. You can feel free to modify them as needed!

Personal and Important Information

I highly recommend creating a special file or box that contains copies of all your family's most important information—birth certificates, marriage certificates, passports, social security cards, titles, insurance records, immunization records, bank and investment records, your will, advanced health directives, and so on. It should also have some basic health information, such as blood type, health issues, or allergies, as well as emergency contact information. Keep your originals in a safe or a locked safety deposit box, where they will be protected in the event of flood, fire, or theft. Having all these important documents in one special place will provide peace of mind and help you avoid stress because you will know exactly where to look for them when you need them.

Bills

Having one dedicated place in your home to sort and pay bills and file your paperwork can be incredibly helpful. However, if you don't have a dedicated home office, you can still set up a portable system that works just as well. Make sure you have all the essentials on hand—calculator, envelopes, stamps, pens, checks, and return address labels. Based on the days your payments are due, pick two or three days per month that will allow you to make sure everything is paid on time, and add bill-paying time as a recurring appointment on your calendar. Use a small bin or basket to collect the bills that need to be paid, then be sure to pay them on your scheduled day. Shred any documents you no longer need, and add any you do need to your "to be filed" box.

Other Paperwork

A high-quality, two-drawer filing cabinet is one of the best investments you can make for your home. Use one drawer to store current paperwork and files, while the other can store archived items like past tax returns and other information you want to keep record of. Set up hanging folders with all of your major categories—insurance, utilities, car payments, credit cards, student loans, mortgage, bank statements, investments, and appliance manuals—and then use manila folders to break down those categories even further. Create a "to be filed" bin for your desk that you can use to collect paperwork throughout the month; then twice a month, right after you pay bills, take a few minutes to file your paperwork.

Kids' Papers

Between tests, homework, worksheets, and artwork, your kids' paperwork can very easily get completely out of control. We've discovered that the simplest solution for our family is open bins placed on a shelf in our girls' closet, one for each of them.

Throughout the school year, any paper they bring home goes straight into the appropriate bin, and when the year is over, we look at everything and decide on a few special items to keep in their keepsake bins while the rest of the items get recycled. Other paperwork, such as announcements from the school, permission slips, and menus, gets dealt with immediately—either signed and returned or added to the calendar.

Calendar and Social Events

I used to keep track of our calendar in a place in our home I called the "control center," which had a wipe board, bulletin board, and dry-erase calendar. While we still use the wipe board and bulletin board to keep track of notes, invitations, and things we don't want to lose (like BookIt coupons), over the years we have transitioned to using primarily an electronic calendar that syncs to our phones. There are lots of different calendar apps to choose from, including some specifically for families. I personally like iCalendar, which syncs with Apple calendar but allows you to make different events different colors. The benefits of using an electronic calendar are that you can set events to repeat, you always have your calendar on hand, and you can set alerts for important events so you don't forget about them. However, I think there is also something to be said for a paper calendar on which you can see everything laid out in front of you. For this, I use a planner I designed called The Purposeful Life Planner™ (available at www.PurposefulLifePlanner.com), which allows me to plan my monthly budget, create weekly meal plans, set goals, and keep track of prayer requests all in one place.

It will be far easier to create a new habit that is more or less a variation or extension of your old habit, rather than trying to initiate an entirely new behavior. Remember, according to Charles Duhigg's *The Power of Habit*, a habit once established in your brain takes very little effort or willpower to maintain. Your brain wants to do the same things over and over. Thus keeping your solutions so simple and easy to remember that they become habits will create success for every member of your family.

Establishing Stricter Limits

By this point, you may have already realized that an essential part of becoming unstuffed is learning to set stricter limits in your life, both in the amount of physical stuff you allow in your home — from books and toys to clothes and more — and in the amount of nonmaterial stuff you allow to cloud up your mind, and take over your time and schedule. Becoming unstuffed means learning to say no to more.

When it comes to paperwork and information overload, sometimes it feels like we don't really have the option to say no. It seems to just come at us, whether or not we want it to, whether or not we accept it. What can we really do about it?

The reality is that, while you may not be able to control every piece of incoming information or every scrap of paper, you can make a conscious effort to cut back on the amount of data that comes your way. You can start by converting all of your bills and payments to auto-pay and opt for digital statements rather than the paper variety. Next, you can unsubscribe to catalogs and junk mail by using a service such as catalogchoice.org. Also, you can cancel subscriptions to magazines or newspapers you never have time to read. These steps alone may easily cut out 90 percent of your incoming mail.

Paper mail is only one area where you can easily set stricter limits. In my own life, for example, I am really bad at listening to my voice mails. My mom especially has a habit of leaving *very* long messages, sometimes as long as ten or fifteen minutes. I generally prefer to call someone back when I've seen that I missed a call rather than taking the time to listen to a long message. As a result, about a year ago, my voice mailbox became completely filled with messages I hadn't yet listened to. When people called, they discovered they couldn't leave a message. So they didn't. They either called back or sent me an email or text message. Living without voice mail was so freeing that I just decided to let my voice mailbox stay full, and it has stayed that way ever since. It is a conscious decision, and I don't feel guilty about it or about the fact that there are still many messages I have never listened to. It may seem like a small thing — and it is — but it has freed my mind from the burden of having to take the time to listen and then respond to one more thing.

Another area where I've had to set strict limits for myself is with Facebook — and especially with Facebook messaging. I refuse to download the Facebook messaging app, and as a general rule, I just don't respond to Facebook messages or to being "tagged" on Facebook, even from my friends. If someone wants to contact me, they can do it via email or text message. My email address is publicly listed in the Contact section at LivingWellSpendingLess.com, which means anyone can find it. I am not preventing or discouraging anyone from contacting me — far from it — but simply setting some personal limits for how and where I can be contacted so I am able to respond without getting overwhelmed and so all my time is not spent trying to keep track of other people's requests. Getting all my messages in one place not only makes life simpler but allows me to respond and follow through more effectively.

I think sometimes we are afraid that setting limits like these will mean we are being mean or thoughtless or stuck-up or self-absorbed, but often it means the opposite. If we don't set strict limits and establish guidelines for ourselves, we end up being washed away by the sea of information, which is of no use to anyone. The reality is that we can better serve others when we have filtered out the unnecessary in favor of the stuff that actually matters the most.

Diving in to Digital Data

I think one of the biggest reasons our "paperwork" feels so oppressive these days is that so much of it is now digital. On top of those physical sheets of paper we constantly shuffle from here to there, there is now also an endless flow of emails, documents, passwords, websites, and digital photographs to contend with. At the rate it continues to pour into our lives and hard drives, it often feels like there is no real way to get a handle on it, no possible way to get ahead. Believe me, I get it. Not only do I spend a large chunk of my time on the computer each day, but at any given time, I generally have no less than ten different projects or blog posts I am working on. It is a lot to keep track of, and if I am not vigilant about sorting it all, I will quickly become stressed and overwhelmed.

I just want to assure you that, while it may feel impossible and will definitely take some time and effort on your part, it is actually possible to take back control of your digital life (or gain it in the first place if you've never had it before!). Applying a few key strategies has really made a difference in my own digital life, and these simple strategies might just help you too.

1. **Set up a junk account.** While it would be great to simply unsubscribe to all junk email, the fact is that if you ever shop online, donate money, or sign up for any sort of freebie, you will inevitably be added to some sort of junk email list—and probably more than one. Thus, I have found it incredibly helpful to have one email address that I can use for these types of sign-ups. It is an account I can access if I need to, but one that I don't have to keep track of on a daily basis. The key

is to use this account *only* for sign-ups and online orders so you never feel obligated to check it.

2. **Keep only unprocessed mail in your inbox.** I have found it enormously helpful to use my main inbox as a to-do list. If it is in my inbox, it still needs to be dealt with in some way, and once I have read, responded, or taken other appropriate action, the email gets archived. I can always tell exactly how much I have to do and who I still need to respond to based on what is in my inbox.

3. **Set up canned responses.** I am a big fan of Gmail, not only because it is free and automatically puts all responses into a single thread, but also because it gives me the ability to set up "canned responses." This is helpful if you are frequently answering the same questions or responding in the same way. For instance, I get a lot of questions about how to start using coupons and about how to start a blog. I am able to respond to these questions quickly and easily because I have a prewritten response ready to go that includes appropriate helpful links and other necessary information. I can still customize the email to fit the exact question being asked, but it just makes things a lot quicker.

4. **Direct all messages to one place.** As I've already discussed, I personally find the ability to send messages in a million different ways incredibly frustrating. However, just because the capability is there doesn't mean you have to live your life that way. Make it clear (in a nice but firm way) that you will only respond to messages sent to your main email address. You can say something like, "Thanks for your message! I would love to respond, but I'm trying to simplify my life by having everything go to one place. Would you mind sending this same message to my email address at *email@email .com?* Thanks so much!" It is clear, to the point, and not at

all offensive. You can even set up a short code in your phone or computer to make your response even quicker. And in the end, anyone who doesn't understand the need to simplify might just be delusional and not worth your time anyway.

5. **Delete spam immediately.** Even after setting up a specific account just for junk mail, you will probably still receive plenty of junk and spam email to your main box. It's everywhere. However, if you make a habit of quickly unsubscribing and then deleting junk and spam mail right away, it will eventually become far less of a problem. If your inbox is already out of control, with hundreds or even thousands of emails, there are a couple of options. You can start over completely with a brand-new email address and just set up auto-responder to let any legitimate friends and family members know your email has changed. Or you can do a mass delete in order to bring your inbox to zero and then hope that if you did accidentally delete something important, whoever it was from will try again. (They usually will.)

6. **Organize your computer desktop.** I personally find electronic documents a lot easier to keep track of than email, especially since moving to an incredibly simple but effective system of computer desktop organization several years ago. I first downloaded a free desktop organizer background image from my friend Heather Moritz at MoritzFineBlogDesigns .com/desktop, and then I created folders for each of my projects, as well as for other things like "business documents," "family photos," and "school info." Documents and photographs automatically get saved to the appropriate folder, and I can always find exactly what I am looking for.

7. **Delete and sort photos as you go.** Digital photography is wonderful but also terrible in many ways. Where we used to be sparing with our twenty-four- or thirty-six-shot rolls of

film, we can now take one hundred shots of the exact same image without having to think twice. While this freedom has certainly given us more chances at the perfect shot, it has also resulted in thousands of photographs where we used to have dozens. I have discovered that the best solution is to delete the not-so-good shots as soon as I upload them, keeping just one or two of the very best photos and discarding the rest. The keepers then go into a labeled folder so I can easily find them again later.

Once again, the key to making any of these solutions actually work for the long term is sticking with it and making it a habit. You *can* take your life back from an informational tidal wave, but you *will* have to work at it. Identify the biggest needs, set up simple systems that work, and then establish filters that tell you exactly how to process the information coming in so you can finally stop procrastinating. Remember, it is not necessarily the paperwork and data that are causing so much stress; rather, it is our inability to process it all. Simplify the process, and you might just find that you've solved the problem.

SAMPLE "IF THIS, THEN THAT" RULES FOR INFORMATION CLUTTER

Creating an information filter—a set of "if this, then that" rules—for all the incoming data in your life is one of the simplest ways to eliminate the stress and feelings of being overwhelmed that come from the sea of paperwork, digital data, and constant need to respond. The following list contains examples of "if this, then that" rules you may want to begin implementing in your own life. You can modify them to fit your unique situations and add rules as needed.

- IF a piece of mail is "junk," THEN it goes directly into the recycling bin.
- IF a piece of mail is a bill that needs to be paid, THEN it goes into the "to be paid" box on my desk. (Bills are paid twice a month.)
- IF a piece of mail is a statement that needs to be filed, THEN it goes into the "to be filed" box on my desk. (This box is emptied twice a month.)
- IF a piece of mail is a personal note or thank-you card, THEN it gets opened, read, and then either saved in a keepsake box (if it is something special) or recycled.
- IF an invitation is received, THEN it gets a decision and a response immediately. If the response is yes, take a picture of the invite, add the event to your calendar, send in your RSVP, and then throw away the invite. If the response is no, send your RSVP, throw away the invite, and move on.
- IF the school sends home a note or menu that needs to be signed, THEN it gets signed immediately and sent back to school the next day.

- IF my kids bring home a test or other work to show me, THEN it gets looked at, commented on, and added to the schoolwork bin on the top shelf of their closet. (This bin gets sorted and emptied at the end of the school year.)
- IF my kids bring home a new piece of artwork, THEN it gets hung in their room until they bring home something new, at which point it gets added to the schoolwork bin at the top of their closet.
- IF I get a spam or junk email I don't want, THEN I will take a second to unsubscribe so I don't get any more messages from that sender.
- IF I get a chain email, THEN I will immediately delete it.
- IF I get an email that needs a response, THEN I will respond as quickly as possible with as brief a response as possible, using a canned response if possible.
- IF I get an email that does not need a response, THEN I will archive it and move on.
- IF I get a text message while I am busy, THEN I will respond during my next break.
- IF I get a Facebook message, THEN I will send a canned response asking the messenger to send me an email instead.
- IF I take a bunch of pictures, THEN I will immediately delete all but the very best.
- IF my computer desktop is messy, THEN I will take a few minutes to drag and drop my files into the appropriate folders.

six

Other People's Stuff

Letting Go of the Guilt

We gather our arms full of guilt as though it were precious stuff. It must be that we want it that way.

John Steinbeck

Every time I write or speak about clutter and the process of getting rid of it, without fail, the most common question I get, and the most common complaint, is "What do I do with all the *other* people's stuff in my life? How do I get rid of *that*?" Through the years, I have discovered, both in my own life and through countless conversations with others, that the hardest things to get rid of are the things that come from other people—the gifts, the heirlooms, and the piles left behind when someone dies. Other people's stuff, it seems, comes attached to a whole lot of guilt.

In the past few years, my husband and I have experienced this phenomenon firsthand. When my mother-in-law died, she left behind a whole house filled with stuff. A child of the Depression, she had a hard time throwing anything away, which meant that much of it—including the endless pile of paperwork—was junk. Even so, there was also a lot that *wasn't* junk—items she had treasured and dreamed of passing on. There was a genuine Lalique crystal vase and a solid silver tea set purchased in Italy during a trip to the Vatican in the 1960s, two full sets of gorgeous (and expensive) fine china, countless collectibles, a few pieces of finely crafted midcentury modern furniture, closets full of old family photographs, and plenty more to sift through.

It took us a week to go through everything to try to determine what we should keep and what we could leave behind. The truth was that we weren't really sure what to do with it—none of it fit our own style or taste—but we felt obligated to take it. After all, this was her life. These were her treasures. We loved Marie very much, and we wanted to honor her in death. What would it say about us if we didn't keep any of her things?

So we kept as much as we could. We packed up a U-Haul shipping container with as many items as it would fit, and then we had it sent back to Florida, where we had to rent a storage unit to hold it all.

Two years later, in what felt very much like a one-two sucker punch, we were faced with another death in the family when my sister-in-law Linda succumbed to a long battle with cancer. It was a devastating loss. With no children of her own, she left everything to my husband and our daughters. While she had been careful to set her financial affairs in order before she died, we were once again faced with the task of sorting through someone's entire life to decide what to keep and what to leave behind.

The guilt was terrible.

You see, Linda was a shopper, and she loved to collect nice things. Her home was beautiful and filled to the brim with her various collections—expensive paintings, Longaberger baskets, Lladró figurines, Halloween decorations, hundreds of pigs in all shapes and sizes, and even a whole dresser full of Silpada jewelry. These collections represented everything she had lived for, and yet they weren't *our* collections or *our* passions. We had no need for them. Our own home was already too full. Even so, it felt like we were literally throwing her life away, and again, we kept far more than we actually wanted.

Again we returned to Florida with boxes and boxes full of stuff. We got an even bigger storage unit.

And it wasn't just the stuff from Linda's own house that we had to contend with; it was all the gifts she had given us over the years. For years, she had showered our girls with elaborate presents—beautiful dresses, customized handmade teepees with matching sleeping bags, a dollhouse, stuffed animals, toys, games and so many things it was almost impossible to keep track of them all. She sent care packages for every minor holiday and hauled suitcases full of gifts to give in person for the major holidays. She truly *loved* my girls, and her way of showing it was with stuff.

Her death hit us hard.

Not surprisingly, my two daughters, who had absolutely adored their auntie, immediately started connecting all the things Linda had given them to still being connected with *her*. Linda and all the stuff she gave them over the years became one and the same. Whenever we wanted to weed out a too-small dress, a no-longer-played-with toy, or a set of ripped pajamas, we were greeted with a flood of tears and shrieks of, "But you *can't* throw that away! *Auntie Linda gave it to us!*"

We realized that our girls were simply doing the same thing we had done, first after my mother-in-law's death and then after Linda's death as well. We were assuming that throwing away someone else's *stuff* meant we were throwing away their *memory*. And we couldn't bear the thought of throwing away someone we loved.

We struggled with this dilemma for a long time until one day, it finally occurred to us that *stuff* and *memories* are not the same thing. If everything is special, then nothing is. The only way we would ever really become unstuffed is to finally give up the guilt.

"YOU CAN'T TAKE IT WITH YOU"

While it may seem a little morbid, thinking about our own possessions in the context of our own inevitable demise may help to serve as the ultimate decluttering motivator.

When I was in high school, our drama department performed the famous play *You Can't Take It with You*, which follows the antics of the lovable but eccentric Sycamore-Vanderhof family. At the climax of the production, the family's patriarch explains to the straitlaced Mr. Kirby, "You can't take it with you, Mr. Kirby, so what good is it? As near as I can see, the only thing you can take with you is the love of your friends."

While I can't say I've always lived my life according to that principle, the older I get, the more I realize the wisdom and truth of those words. Of course, this is not exactly a new concept. In Luke 12:16–21, Jesus tells the parable of the rich fool:

"The ground of a certain rich man yielded an abundant harvest. He thought to himself, 'What shall I do? I have no place to store my crops.'

"Then he said, 'This is what I'll do. I will tear down my barns and build bigger ones, and there I will store my surplus grain. And I'll say to myself, "You have plenty of grain laid up for many years. Take life easy; eat, drink and be merry."

"But God said to him, 'You fool! This very night your life will be demanded from you. Then who will get what you have prepared for yourself?'

"This is how it will be with whoever stores up things for themselves but is not rich toward God."

The point of the story is pretty clear: Our stuff can't save us. In the end, every single one of us will die, and chances are, most of what we leave behind will be nothing but a burden to the people we love. Harsh? Maybe. But true.

If you are struggling to let go of your excess stuff, why not consider taking a different tack and looking at it in terms of eternity? You really *can't* take it with you, but the people you leave behind will be forced to deal with it. What sort of legacy do you want to leave behind? Memories—or stuff?

Why Do We Feel So Guilty?

Guilt is a powerful motivator and a powerful presence in most of our lives. According to a recent article in *Psychology Today*, we spend, on average, about five hours per week feeling guilty. While a little guilt can be good—helping us to protect our relationships even when we don't necessarily feel like it—it can also be a big disruption in our lives, making it difficult for us to think straight, making us more reluctant to enjoy life, causing us to avoid others, and also making us feel resentful and "heavy."[9] In other words, guilt can weigh on us like a heavy chain around our neck.

When it comes to decluttering and letting stuff go, there are many different reasons we might feel guilty, and not all of them have to do specifically with other people's stuff; some have to do with our own insecurities and shortcomings. These include:

- *Feeling wasteful.* This is the guilt that occurs when we don't want to throw something away that might still be useful because it feels like a waste. This type of guilt is often accompanied with the words, "But I might use that someday."
- *Financial guilt.* Closely tied to guilt about feeling wasteful, financial guilt comes from not wanting to get rid of something because it was expensive or because "good money was spent"

on it. It feels like throwing money away, and so we keep something we don't really want.

- *Sentimentality.* This is the guilt that gets attached to objects associated with happy memories. A little girl's favorite dress, a drawer full of birthday cards, a box full of old trophies. This guilt often asks, "How could I ever get rid of that when it meant so much?"
- *Not wanting to hurt others.* This is one of the most common types of guilt to get attached to the stuff that comes from other people, especially gifts. We don't want to hurt anyone's feelings, particularly people we really care about, and so we hang on to the things we've been given, regardless of whether they are still useful or even something we enjoy. "But it was a gift!" becomes the primary reason for not letting something go.
- *Unrealized goals.* This is the guilt that gets attached to the stuff associated with projects and hobbies, unused sporting equipment, clothes that no longer fit, books we haven't finished, or anything else we've meant to do but haven't (and probably won't). We hang on to this type of stuff because we feel guilty about having failed and instead prefer to cling to an unrealistic optimism that "someday" we'll get to it.
- *Parental guilt.* This is the guilt that gets tied to our kids' stuff, and often this one is a doozy, especially when we, as parents, are the primary sources of the excess stuff. This type of guilt manifests itself in many different ways. One such way is guilt over not having enough time or energy for our kids, and making up for it by buying them things. Another is guilt over wanting to create the perfect childhood, and again filling their life with stuff. In both cases, and many others, the justification for both providing the excess of stuff and then not wanting to get rid of it is, "I just want my kids to be happy."
- *Memory guilt.* As we've already mentioned, this is the guilt that gets attached to the things left behind from people who are no

longer in our lives, whether it's a relationship that fell apart, a friend who moved away, or the death of a loved one. We don't want to get rid of it because it feels like we might be throwing away our memory of that person as well.

So many different types of guilt, all resulting in essentially the same problem — a reluctance and unwillingness or inability to simply let things go. And so we find ourselves stuck in an endless cycle of guilt and stuff. The guilt causes us to keep things we don't want, which in turn causes us to feel guilty about all the stuff we still have. We don't want to let it go, but we don't want to keep it either.

So what's the solution?

Separating the Memories from the Stuff

In my own family, eventually all four of us had to come to grips with the fact that hanging on to the piles of stuff Linda had given us — every single fancy silk dress, special toy, blanket, basket, figurine, card, piece of jewelry, and funny singing Hallmark stuffed animal — would not bring her back. Even more importantly, we had to come to accept the hard truth that by equating the person she had been with the stuff she had given us, we were only diminishing and cheapening her memory, not retaining it. Not everything can be special.

The reality was that Linda was *so much more* than all the silly stuff she left us with! If we really wanted to honor her memory, we needed to do so by remembering the person she had been, the love she had shown, and the impact she had made, not just as an auntie and sister, but as a school principal and community leader, as a daughter and cousin and friend. If we wanted to honor her memory, we could talk about our favorite funny stories, the laughs we shared, the tears we cried, even the fights and frustrations.

Actually letting go of all the stuff has been an ongoing process, one we've had to tackle a little at a time. We still have a storage unit we would like to be rid of completely someday. For now, we are content to tackle it in small bites.

I don't think my family is alone in this struggle to separate the people we love from the stuff they leave behind or to separate a favorite memory from the stuff that gets attached to the memory. And as we just saw, this guilt doesn't just happen in death either, though death can certainly amplify the guilt.

The only real solution is to learn how to make a clear distinction between our memories and our stuff. In order to give up the guilt that causes us to hold on tight to other people's stuff, we have to first reset our thinking. We have to accept, at our core, the fundamental truth that *people and things are not one and the same.*

Consider this:

Memories take up space in our hearts; *stuff takes up space in our homes.*

Memories last forever; *stuff breaks, gets lost, and fades away.*

Memories bring joy; *stuff brings stress.*

Memories are honoring; *stuff is diminishing.*

Memories bring peace; *stuff brings chaos.*

Memories actually matter; *stuff really doesn't matter at all.*[*]

The sooner we can make this mind-set shift and stop equating other people's memories with the stuff they leave behind, the sooner we can give ourselves permission to stop clinging to the things we don't need or even really want, simply because we feel that without them, we are losing the person we loved. That's no small feat.

Chances are that this mind-set shift won't happen overnight either, especially for those of us who have held on to this guilt for a very long time. It's not always easy to accept the thought that just because we might be letting go of their stuff, we are not actually letting go of that person. But the simple fact we must continue to remind ourselves of,

---

[*] For instructions on how to access a printable version of this list, see page 219 at the back of the book.

especially when the guilt starts to creep in, is that memories and stuff are not the same.

Memories and stuff are not the same.

Dealing with Gifts

Of course, even if we manage to purge ourselves of the guilt we've attached to our *existing* stuff, there will still be birthdays and holidays and just-because days that bring new gifts — and a fresh wave of guilt. Even when we've done our best to minimize the number of unwanted items in our lives, there will be times when we find ourselves on the receiving end of something we'd really just rather do without. So what do we do? Is there a way to gracefully decline a gift without completely destroying our relationships? How do we balance gratitude with our desire to become unstuffed?

If only there were easy, clear-cut answers to these questions! The reality is that gifts — both the expectation of giving and the process of receiving — can cause any number of sticky, uncomfortable situations. And while there may not be hard-and-fast rules, keeping the following strategies in mind can help make navigating these muddy waters a little easier:

1. **Be gracious.** While deep down, you may not feel all that excited about dealing with yet one more thing, your first job as the recipient of a gift is to show graciousness to the giver and respond with a heartfelt "thank you." Even if the gift seriously missed the mark, you can be grateful for the fact that they remembered you and that you were important enough to them to take the time to pick out a gift. An attitude of genuine gratitude will make everything else easier and help pave the way for anything else you may decide to do.

2. **Be open but not obnoxious.** It is perfectly acceptable to be open and honest with your friends and family members about your gift preferences, as long as you can be open in a way that is not obnoxious or rude. Let friends and family members know, in a nonconfrontational and nonaccusatory way, that you are trying to cut back on stuff and would really prefer no gifts. For instance, if your parents are asking about your son's birthday, you could say something like, "We've been trying really hard to take the focus off of gifts and focus instead on experiences and people. If you want to give Charlie a gift for his birthday, would you mind making it something he can do with you rather than a toy?" Likewise, for my own daughters' birthday parties, we have instituted a strict policy of no gifts, including a note in the invitations that reads, "Your presence is your present; please, no gifts! (All gifts will be donated to Toys for Tots!) Thank you!" My husband and I have learned to be more open with each other, as well as with our kids, and to be clear that our focus is on the experiences, not the presents. One other option, for those gift givers who really prefer to give an object, is to request something consumable, such as gourmet foods, bath items, candles, flowers, essential oils, or specialty cleaning products. For kids, you might request consumables such as markers, crayons, paint sets, bubbles, and so on.

3. **Be creative.** Chances are that even when you've been perfectly open about your gift preferences, you will still find yourself on the receiving end of a gift you don't really want. That's when it may be time to get a little creative. An article in *Real Simple*'s online magazine quotes interior designer Maxwell Gillingham-Ryan: "When you receive a present, your duty is to receive it and thank the giver, not to hold on to it forever."[10] Truer words were never spoken. We are duty-bound to show gratitude, but rather than keep something you don't want or

need, a better option is to find something useful to do with the object, whether you return it to the store and use the credit for something you will enjoy more, sell it, or re-gift it to someone you know who will actually use and appreciate the object.

HOW TO GRACIOUSLY DECLINE A GIFT

Saying no to a gift without hurting the giver's feelings can definitely be challenging, and in many—perhaps even most—cases, it might just be better to say thank you and move on. That said, here are a few tactics you may want to try if someone gives you something you really don't want, need, or feel comfortable accepting.

1. **For hand-me-down toys, clothes, etc.:** "Thank you so much for your thoughtfulness, but we have actually been trying to cut way back on our toy/clothing/whatever collection! We have found a great charity to donate them to—would you like me to give you the name?"

2. **For expensive items:** "Wow, thank you so much, but I'm afraid this is far too generous! I really appreciate your thoughtfulness, but I'm just not comfortable accepting something so valuable."

3. **For inappropriate items or things you don't approve of:** "Thank you so much! I know you didn't know this, but we actually don't allow X in our house, so I am afraid we are going to have to decline. I really appreciate the thought, though."

4. **For something you absolutely hate:** "Oh, _____, thank you so much for thinking of me! I'm so touched, but I couldn't possibly accept this right now. Do you have anyone else in mind you could give it to?"

4. **Be discreet.** While you shouldn't feel guilty about finding a creative use for the gift you've received, it is a sign of graciousness, politeness, and maturity to be discreet about your creativity. Don't make it common knowledge that you hated a gift or say anything publicly that might disparage the giver. If you feel the need to tell him or her that you didn't keep the gift, do it privately.

5. **Be kind.** There may be times when you know someone would be genuinely hurt if you didn't keep the gift they gave you. Remember, there are no hard-and-fast rules when it comes to this type of situation, and decluttering is not an absolute science. It is perfectly okay to make an exception to spare someone's feelings.

6. **Put the shopper to work.** Often the gift giver in the family is a person who really enjoys shopping. If so, feed them ideas throughout the year of things they can keep an eye out for — things your family really needs, such as clothing, seasonal items, and so on. That way you help them scratch their shopping itch and also take the burden off of yourself to do all the family shopping.

7. **Be a trendsetter.** Why not be the person in your circle of friends or within your family to change the gift-giving policies that have become tradition? Will your Christmas gathering be ruined if you don't do a gift exchange, or could you find something else to take its place? Could you start a trend of going out for lunch to celebrate a birthday rather than exchanging gifts each year? Old patterns sometimes die hard, but they will never change unless you are willing to step up and be the person who makes the change.

Gifts can be a wonderful blessing, but they can also become a serious burden when they fill up our lives with stuff we don't really need or want but feel too guilt-ridden to get rid of. The reality is that, depending on what kind of people you are dealing with in your life — especially if you have parents or in-laws who simply refuse to heed your requests for less — gift giving (and receiving) may *always* be somewhat of a sticky subject. When in doubt, show grace, both to the giver and to yourself. Be mindful of their motives — Are they consciously trying to irritate you, or is this just how they express their affection? — and your own as well. (Is this person someone you are easily irritated with or with whom you have a history of disagreement?) Proverbs 15:1 tells us, "A gentle answer turns away wrath, but a harsh word stirs up anger." When we approach each sticky gift situation from a place of tenderness and love instead of blindly insisting on having our own way, we might just find we can eventually find some common ground and maintain the relationship in the process. People will always be more important than stuff.

Letting It Go, Once and for All

It's not easy to give up the guilt that gets attached to so much of our stuff in so many different ways. In fact, when it comes to decluttering and becoming truly unstuffed, this mental battle with ourselves is far more difficult than the actual physical process of filling up a bunch of boxes and garbage bags with all the stuff we no longer use or want. We want to be free of the clutter in our homes, but we are just as desperate to be free of the weight of the guilt attached to all these items.

So how do we let it go, once and for all?

How do we rid ourselves not only of the physical mess but of the mental distress that comes along with it? Is it really possible to stop feeling guilty about how we've filled our garages, basements, attics, and closets with so much stuff we simply don't need? To stop caring about the gifts we feel bad for not wanting? To stop torturing ourselves about the ways we've failed as parents? To stop beating ourselves up over the unfulfilled dreams and missed opportunities? Can we actually get rid of things we've inherited without feeling like we are throwing someone else's life away? Can we really, truly hold on to the memories without holding on to the stuff?

I believe we can.

Here's the thing—as humans, we have plenty to feel guilty about. In fact, we probably *should* feel guilty. As a general rule, we are all a mess. I don't know about you, but I fail daily in a million different ways. We are all fallen, desperate, damaged, and deeply flawed creatures in need of nothing but grace—a grace we have already been freely given, *despite the fact that we don't deserve it at all*. As Romans 3:23–24 puts it, "For *all* have sinned and fall short of the glory of God, and all are *justified freely by his grace* through the redemption that came by Christ Jesus" (emphasis added).

And there is nothing we can do to change it. It has already been done. We've been washed clean. Completely blemish-free. A new creation. In fact, according to 2 Corinthians 5:17, "The old has gone, the new is here!"

In other words, we've already been unstuffed.

So absolving ourselves from the comparatively insignificant guilt of too much stuff? I'd say that's definitely doable.

Here are a few concrete strategies that might help you break free of the guilt that is paralyzing you, and finally help you get rid of all those items you've been hanging on to:

1. **Change the tape.** Start by switching out the guilt messages that play over and over in your brain, the ones that insist you can't get rid of something because of the potentially catastrophic consequences. Understand that these messages have probably been deeply ingrained into your psyche, which means changing them will take a lot of effort and repetition! Different tapes will be required for each of the different types of guilt:

- **Feeling wasteful.** Instead of saying, "But I might use that someday," tell yourself it is better that someone else be able to use it right now.
- **Financial guilt.** Instead of saying, "But I spent good money on that," or, "I'm throwing money away," tell yourself that the money is already gone. Better to sell it and recoup some of the loss than to keep it and get nothing out of it.
- **Sentimentality.** Instead of saying, "This means too much to get rid of," take a picture and remind yourself that memories and objects are not the same thing.
- **Not wanting to hurt others.** Instead of saying, "But it was a gift," remind yourself that your only obligation is to sincerely thank the giver. If that has been done, you are free to find a new home for the gift.
- **Unrealized goals.** Instead of saying, "But I might finish that or get to that someday," give yourself permission to give up on a dream. Remind yourself that sometimes it is okay to fail and that failure often opens the door to new opportunities we otherwise may have missed.
- **Parental guilt.** Instead of telling yourself that "this will make up for my not being there," or, "I just want my kids to be happy," remind yourself that more stuff will not make happier kids but instead will create discontented and spoiled kids. Kids need boundaries and limits — they crave them. Don't let guilt fool you into trying to buy their happiness. It won't work.
- **Memory guilt.** Instead of telling yourself, "But it feels like I am throwing away someone's memory," remind yourself that by equating someone's memory with the stuff they left behind, you are actually diminishing and cheapening their memory. Remember the ones you've loved by treasuring *who they were*, not what they had.

2. **Decide to decide.** In one of my favorite books on getting organized, *The Organizing Sourcebook*, author Kathy Waddill offers nine practical strategies for simplifying your life. Her strategy #7 is to "decide to decide." Of this strategy, she wisely writes, "When a major life event occurs—tragic or joyful—it puts people in a state of flux. If you don't know what life is going to look like tomorrow, it's hard to make decisions today … The net result of postponed decisions is that things start to pile up … As soon as you make up your mind to do something, things will begin to happen. It is the *decision to act* that causes an action to occur. Without the decision, nothing will happen, and nothing will get better."[11] In other words, the act of decluttering and throwing things away, *even if we feel guilty about it*, can actually cause us to feel *less* guilty over time. The feelings follow the action. All we have to do is decide to act.

3. **Set limits before you begin.** Examining your items one at a time makes it easy to justify keeping more than you should. Chances are that every single item has a corresponding excuse, a reason to be kept. And taken one at a time, it may not even seem so bad. After all, it is just one thing, right? The problem, of course, is that each of those single, seemingly harmless items adds up quickly to one big problem. Thus, a better approach is to set limits before you begin on how much you will keep. These limits can be applied to everything, including clothing, housewares, knickknacks, photographs, and more. Decide ahead of time what is a reasonable quantity to keep, and then keep no more. And as you do your sorting, Marie Kondo of *The Life-Changing Magic of Tidying Up* advises you to deal with categories of items all at one time— all your books, all your knickknacks, all your jewelry, and so on.[12] This helps your brain look at the problem as a whole instead of dividing it up into different parts (which might cause you to keep more than you should).

4. **Do it scared.** If you wait until you're ready, until you feel nothing but wonderful and completely unburdened by the idea of decluttering and getting rid of the things you've felt too guilty to let go, you may be waiting a very long time. Sometimes you just have to do it even when you're scared. As I frequently tell my daughters, courage doesn't mean you're never scared. It means being scared and doing it anyway. Eleanor Roosevelt said it even better: "You gain strength, courage and confidence by every experience in which you really stop to look fear in the face. You are able to say to yourself, 'I have lived through this horror. I can take the next thing that comes along.' ... *You must do the thing you think you cannot do.*"[13] So just do it.

5. **Get help.** And if you really don't think you can do it? Find someone — perhaps a close friend, a sister, or even a professional organizer — who can help you make decisions, set reasonable limits, and change the guilt tapes that are playing in the back of your mind. You'd be amazed at what a second, more objective opinion can do!

In the end, learning to give up the guilt we've attached to so much of the stuff filling up our lives is a lifelong process, one that likely won't be without its setbacks. We have to begin by recognizing those triggers that make us feel guilty in the first place, whether it's financial guilt, sentimentality, or something else. We also have to learn how to separate out our memories from the items we've attached those memories to, and then to accept the truth that memories and stuff are not the same thing. We've got to develop strategies for dealing with the influx of other people's stuff, especially gifts, and finally, we have to learn how to let go of the guilt, once and for all, by changing the tapes that have played for too long, by finally deciding to decide, and by doing it scared.

It's no small task, but it is possible.

Why not start today?

CLEARING OUT A LIFETIME OF STUFF

Dealing with the physical objects a parent, spouse, or other close family member has left behind can be incredibly challenging, especially when you are simultaneously dealing with the emotions and grief of losing a loved one. What are you supposed to do with it all? How do you retain your memories of a person without hanging on to all the stuff they've left you? While there are no easy answers or any one-size-fits-all plan, here are a few practical tips you can use when faced with inheriting someone else's lifetime of possessions.

1. **Get support.** When you are reeling from the loss of someone you loved, it might feel too painful or overwhelming to begin sifting through a lifetime of memories all alone. Don't be afraid to ask for help, perhaps from a close friend, sibling, or maybe an acquaintance who has been through this before. Having someone by your side who isn't also grieving can help keep you on track and allow you to be more objective. Try to choose someone who is a good organizer or good at getting things done.

2. **Choose a few special items to keep.** Sorting through someone else's entire lifetime of stuff, especially through their collections, mementos, and keepsakes, can very easily make us feel obligated to keep more than we actually want or can even use. As Chuck put it after Linda died, "It feels like I am throwing her life away." In the end, however, we will feel much closer to the person whose memories we are trying to preserve if we can select just a few very special items to remember them by—perhaps one special piece of jewelry, a photo album they made, or even a piece of furniture they loved.

3. **Pace yourself.** If you can, try to give yourself enough time to sort through everything, taking breaks as needed when it gets too hard or too emotional.

4. **Let it go.** Once you've selected which mementos or keepsakes you want to hold on to or to pass to other friends or family members, it is time to sell or donate the rest. Thankfully, a number of organizations and companies can help make this process much easier:

- *Estate sale companies.* This is probably the easiest, most painless option, though you will have to pay for the convenience. An estate sale company will come to your home, determine what is valuable, organize it, sell it, and then get rid of the remaining items. You don't have to do anything ahead of time to prepare—they generally prefer that you don't—and when they are finished, the house will be completely clear. The fees for this service vary, though it is generally somewhere in the range of 10 to 30 percent of all proceeds from the sale.

- *eBay companies.* If your loved one is leaving behind valuable keepsakes or collections, you may want to consider contacting a professional eBay seller to list them for you. As a general rule, you will have to do the work of dropping off the items you want to sell, but you may be able to get a better price for the items than you would from an estate sale.

- *Specialty items.* You may want to take any specialty items such as antiques, coins, guns, jewelry, or baseball cards to a dealer or expert in that field.

- *Donations.* For items you don't wish to bother selling, there are a number of charities that will schedule home pickup, including the Salvation Army and Goodwill. Simply contact your local store for more details.

PART THREE

Soul

seven

Friends

Cultivating Real Relationships

*Friendship ... is born at that moment when one man
says to another "What! You too? I thought that no
one but myself..."*

C. S. Lewis

That moment we met is so ingrained in my memory that it feels
like it just happened. It was January 2011 at the opulent and massive Gaylord Opryland Resort and Convention Center in Nashville. If
you've never been there, it is a sight to behold. One of the largest hotels
and convention centers in the world, the hotel is practically a small city,
with nearly three thousand rooms; dozens of restaurants, shops, and
atriums; and even its own jungle, island, and canal system. Getting
lost—like I did on the first day—can mean wandering around for an
hour or more. Needless to say, I was a little bit intimidated.

I was a brand-new blogger at my very first blogging conference.
Having just started my tiny little blog only six months before, I knew
nothing and no one, and I arrived feeling hopelessly lost and desperately insecure. My notebook and pen looked downright foolish next
to all the shiny silver MacBook Pros and brand-new iPads, and while
everyone else tweeted away on their iPhones and talked about "following the Twitter stream," I quietly wondered what the heck a hashtag
was and hoped no one would notice the non-smart phone in my pocket

or the fact that I had *no idea* what they were talking about. I was so out of my league that I hadn't even booked a room at the right hotel. Convincing my husband to let me come had meant finding the cheapest hotel option available. I had to take the free shuttle to the Gaylord, which meant being dropped off on the opposite side of the property from where the conference was taking place. (Hence the getting lost.)

I finally found the registration desk, got signed in, and tried not to look as intimidated as I felt, wandering around this room full of laughing, animated, and very confident-looking women. I edged my way closer to a group of friendly-looking gals, praying I would look like I fit in and just hoping they wouldn't shun me or ask me to leave.

As I stood there awkwardly, silently willing *someone* to talk to me, I suddenly saw a familiar face walking right toward me. It was my blogging hero. The person whose blog had inspired me to start my own. The person whose blog I checked at least several times a day, the one in whose forums I was a very active participant. And there she was, this rock star, this *giant*, walking my way.

I couldn't stop myself. As she walked by, not even noticing me, I called out, almost involuntarily, "Oh my gosh, you're *so and so*! I *love* your blog!"

She stopped and slowly looked me up and down appraisingly, not smiling at all.

"What's your name?" she asked.

I told her who I was and my blog name, and a flicker of recognition crossed her face.

"Oh," she said, still not smiling, her tone making it clear she was not impressed. "I know exactly who you are. You leave a *lot* of comments, don't you?"

I have never in my life prayed harder for the floor to open up and swallow me whole. Of course it didn't. The superstar blogger turned and walked away, making it clear I wasn't worth her time, and I tried desperately to hold myself together until I was at least out of the room. I burst into the hallway, wanting nothing more than to catch the shuttle back to my hotel, leave that place, and never come back. Blogging was clearly not for me.

But in the hallway, all by herself, stood *another* blogger I recognized. In fact, in my rush to exit, I almost ran her over. Edie was also a rock star in the blogging world, but a rock star who had recently suffered a major tragedy. Just four weeks earlier and only a few days before Christmas, Edie and her family had lost everything they owned in a devastating house fire. They barely escaped with their lives. She had come to the conference because she had purchased a ticket months beforehand, but she was still reeling from the catastrophe. Like thousands of other readers, I had been closely following her story, captivated by her raw, gut-wrenching posts. Her grief was so transparent.

I was shocked to see her standing there, and again, I involuntarily blurted out, "Oh my gosh, you're Edie!" It was a statement, not a question.

I don't know what I was expecting, but the minute she looked at me, I could tell that she *saw* me, and I burst into tears.

And then *she* burst into tears.

We were both a mess.

When we finally managed to stop crying, she asked, in her sweet Southern drawl, "Oh honey, are you here all by yourself? Then you can just hang out with me."

I hadn't yet said a word. There was no way for her to know.

She proceeded to write down her cell phone number, and also tell me the names of the friends she was with, just in case she wasn't around. I was stunned. Despite everything that was going on in her life, despite the fact that she was in the midst of a personal crisis, despite the fact that she was already an incredibly popular blogger and an established member of the Blissdom inner circle, and despite the fact that everyone at the conference was rallying to support *her*, she saw *me*. If there was ever a time when a person would be legitimately justified in being self-absorbed, it was *that* moment.

But she saw *me*.

And thus begun a most beautiful friendship, one that has not only endured through the past five years but grown stronger, richer, and deeper with time. We've celebrated each other's successes, cried over our mistakes, talked each other down from the ledge when necessary, and provided more pep talks than I can count. As accountability partners, we not only encourage one another but also challenge each other when necessary. She knows the parts of me that I often keep hidden — the insecurity, the frustration, the self-doubt, and the pain of past hurts — and I know hers.

And it all started there in that hallway as I was trying to escape, because she was willing to overlook her own pain to notice someone else's.

What Does a Real Relationship Look Like?

It may seem odd in a book about decluttering to spend a chapter focusing on relationships and friendships. But in much the same way as we have filled our homes with piles and piles of stuff we don't need or even really want, and in much the same way as we have filled our minds with the stress of an overstuffed schedule and guilt over letting go, many of us have cluttered our spirits with superficial and toxic relationships. These so-called friendships seem to suck the life out of us rather than nurture our souls.

A big part of the problem is that we often base our relationships on what we think we can *get* out of the relationship rather than on what we are willing to put into it. Although it seems counterintuitive, the more we try to get out of the relationship, the more the relationship sucks the life out of us. We all want relationships that are going to make us feel good about ourselves, that are going to make us feel loved and accepted and nourished, but, according to that famous passage found in 1 Corinthians 13:4–8, it's quite possible we've got it all backward:

> Love is patient, love is kind. It does not envy, it does not boast, it is not proud. It does not dishonor others, it is not self-seeking, it is not easily angered, it keeps no record of wrongs. Love does not delight in evil but rejoices with the truth. It always protects, always trusts, always hopes, always perseveres.
>
> Love never fails.

Real relationships aren't based on what we can *get*, but on what we can *give*.

So what does that look like? How do we know whether or not the relationships in our lives, whether with family members, friends, or even spouses, are where they should be? How can we be sure we are cultivating and nourishing genuine, healthy, life-giving relationships in our day-to-day lives?

Here are the essential qualities we should be looking for, not necessarily in others, but in *ourselves*:

- **Patience.** According to the dictionary, to be patient means "quietly and steadily persevering or diligent, especially in detail or exactness." In a world that moves increasingly fast, patience is a virtue that is often very difficult to come by. But real relationships take time, and they also don't mind waiting. Are you treating your relationships with the patience they deserve? Are you willing to wait, even when you don't feel like it, or are you constantly rushing? Do you savor your moments together, or do you feel like there is never enough time?

- **Kindness.** Real relationships are gentle and tender, where we always treat each other with respect. Do you build up your friends and family members rather than tear them down? Are you slow to criticize or shoot from the hip, and instead choose your words carefully? Are you *nice*? Is your default set on kindness rather than on snarkiness?

- **Absence of jealousy.** Nothing can destroy a relationship faster than the presence of the green-eyed monster. If we're not careful, those feelings of jealousy can easily creep up on us and take over our thoughts, causing deep-seated discontentment and clouding our view of the people we love. Are you struggling with feeling envious of your friends or siblings? Do you find yourself wanting what they have, or are you content with your own lot in life? Do you resent their success, or are you genuinely happy for their triumphs?

- **Humility.** My dad used to joke, "It's hard to be humble when you're as great as I am!" And while he may have been only joking, the reality is that many of us spend a great deal of time tooting our own horns, bragging, and trying to build ourselves up in front of others. Whether this need to make ourselves bigger or more important than we are comes from a place of insecurity or one of haughtiness, the end result is the same. When it comes to your own relationships, are you quick to bring attention to yourself, or do you turn the focus to others? Are you ever guilty of false humility — pretending to be humble in a way that actually brings attention or glory to yourself? Does your insecurity sometimes cause you to brag or boast, even though you later wish you hadn't?

- **Selflessness.** It can sometimes take a whole lot of effort in a relationship to not make it all about *you* — your feelings, your desires, your needs. But selflessness means putting someone else's needs ahead of your own and thinking about someone else's feelings and desires first, *before* you think about your own. This is a daunting requirement, but in *real* relationships, selflessness shouldn't feel painful, because we actually care deeply about the people whose needs we are putting above our own.

- **Graciousness.** In its most basic form, graciousness simply means being willing to give people the benefit of the doubt. One of my favorite quotes comes from Irving Becker: "If you don't like someone, the way he holds his spoon will make you furious. If you care about someone, he can turn his plate over in your lap and you won't mind." I love that quote because it reminds me so much of something I already know to be true — when I don't really like someone, everything they do is annoying! But graciousness is the opposite of that — it assumes the best about other people's motives rather than the worst. Do you show grace in your relationships? Are you quick to judge or become annoyed, or are you willing to give people the benefit of the doubt, even when they've done something to offend you?

• **Forgiveness.** While graciousness means giving someone the benefit of the doubt to avoid becoming angry or offended in the first place, forgiveness means being willing to let go of *actual* offenses. When it comes to real relationships, the ability to forgive and forget is not just important; it is *essential*. In your own relationships, do you frequently hold a grudge, or are you willing to let bygones be bygones? Do you harbor resentment and bitterness for past wrongs, or do you truly let things go and move on? Are you quick to say, "I forgive you," and mean it, or do those words never seem to come? In addition, are you able to admit fault and seek forgiveness, or do you cover up, close up, or close down? Sometimes being forgiven can be just as painful, if not more so, than forgiving, because it forces you to come face-to-face with your own failings.

• **Honesty.** A relationship that is not built on truthfulness is a relationship that is doomed from the start. Real relationships are honest, even when honesty is hard. Are you a truth teller in your relationship, or do you skate over facts in favor of what is easy or pleasant? Have you been honest about your own misdeeds, or do you lie to keep others from knowing what you've done? Do you choose flattery over honesty, or are you willing to speak up when necessary, even if your opinion might not be popular?

- **Protectiveness.** Real relationships protect and shelter those who are in them. Do you look out for your friends and family members and do what you can to keep them safe from harm? Are you willing to jump in and defend them against attack? Do you take it personally when someone comes after them, or are you quick to turn away and say, "That's not really my problem"? Do you protect and shelter the people you love?

- **Trustworthiness.** Becoming someone whom others can really trust, wholly and completely, is no small feat. According to the dictionary, to be trustworthy means to be "deserving of trust or confidence; dependable; reliable." Are you truly trustworthy? Do you deserve the trust and confidence of others? Do you live your life with integrity? Do you avoid gossiping and talking about others? Can you keep a secret? Do you keep your promises?

- **Perseverance.** Real relationships endure, even when the road gets rough. A real friend is in it for the long haul, and understands that there may be some big bumps and potholes along the way. Are you willing to persevere, even when your relationships get hard, even when your friends and family members let you down or disappoint you? Are you willing to keep going, or are you quick to throw in the towel?

Real relationships are tricky and messy and sticky and hard. They take effort and endurance and selflessness and yes, lots of perseverance. Even scarier, real relationships make us vulnerable. Putting ourselves out there — taking the first step of changing our own attitude toward relationships — also means opening ourselves up to the possibility of being hurt, of having our tender hearts trampled on, of being taken advantage of or betrayed. But real relationships are also what make life so rich. They are the foundation of a meaningful life, the thing that keeps us going when times get tough. They are the people who will celebrate your triumphs with you and cry with you when you fall. They are the people who will love you no matter what. With great risk comes great reward, and while the effort of cultivating real relationships may feel risky, the reward is worth it.

Eliminating Superficiality and Toxic Relationships

While real relationships are worth the risk, it is also important to recognize the reality that not every friendship or acquaintanceship can or should be a *real* relationship. As we've just seen, real relationships take time, effort, and a willingness to be vulnerable. Few of us have the energy or mental capacity for even a handful of deep, meaningful relationships, much less dozens. And yet we often forgo quality for quantity. We eagerly accept little more than superficiality, collecting friends on Facebook instead of in real life, sharing and reading only the heavily edited highlights and then measuring our worth and popularity by the number of likes or comments we receive. We allow toxic relationships to choke out the meaningful ones, and instead of cultivating real relationships, we settle for skin-deep.

And these superficial, toxic relationships are taking their toll. According to an article in *Psychology Today*, toxic relationships can lead to stress, anxiety, and even health problems. In fact, in a long-term study, researchers discovered that subjects in negative relationships were far more likely to develop cardiac problems than those in healthy relationships.[14] Furthermore, toxic relationships can raise your blood pressure, lower your immune system, cause chronic headaches, affect your sleep patterns, and even cause depression and weight gain.[15] Meanwhile, a study at the University of Arizona found that superficial relationships on social media do nothing to alleviate feelings of loneliness and can actually compound them, leading to increased feelings of detachment.[16]

So how do we stop settling for superficiality? How do we eliminate these toxic, shallow, inconsequential interactions from our lives, the ones that eat up our time and energy but don't actually contribute to our well-being? The ones that make us second-guess our own worth or spend copious amounts of time trying to impress people we don't even really like? The ones that drain our energy, elevate our blood pressure, and damage our health? How do we *unstuff* our relationships? After all, we can't just throw *people* away.

Can we?

For the record, the answer is no. We can't—and shouldn't—throw people away. Nor should we become so consumed by the need to eliminate superficial relationships in our life that we forget to show compassion, kindness, and grace. It is a delicate and sometimes tricky balance to strike, but that doesn't mean it is impossible. Eliminating the toxic and superficial connections in favor of real relationships means first being able to identify the areas of concern and then establishing (and sticking to) clear boundaries.

Here are some red flags of a toxic or superficial relationship to watch out for:

1. **Jealousy.** Do you often feel jealous or envious of this person, or does he or she often seem jealous or envious of you? Do you ever find yourself secretly wishing he or she would fail or have something bad happen, or do you ever feel like he or she is wishing *you* would fail?

2. **Insecurity.** Does being around this person or being exposed to this person on social media make you feel bad about yourself? Do you question your own self-worth or try to boost your own ego when around this person? Does this person seem insecure around you? Do they frequently boast, brag, or puff themselves up to try to look good?

3. **Surfacey.** Does this relationship go deep, or does it stay only on the surface? Do you feel like you can really be yourself around this person? Do you feel like you are free to change

around this person? Does this person feel comfortable going deep with you? Can they be themselves around you? Do you talk about real issues, or are you only forever exchanging pleasantries? Do you get together in real life, or is your contact limited to online only?

4. **Guilt.** Does being around this person make you feel guilty about something or someone? Does this person feel guilty when he or she is around you? Do you feel like you are not living up to the obligations or expectations set by this person, or are you setting unreasonable expectations for him or her?

5. **Criticism.** Is this relationship prone to an excess of criticism, either by you or about you? Do you feel like you can't do anything right when you are with this person? Does he or she feel like they can't do anything right when they are with you?

6. **Feeling of being used.** Do you give more than you receive in this relationship, or is your relationship, for the most part, balanced? Are you resentful of the demands this friend puts on you or on your time? Does he or she respect your limits?

7. **Abuse.** Is this relationship physically, sexually, or emotionally abusive in any way? If so, please get help right away by talking to a trusted friend, coworker, parent, or pastor.

Setting Boundaries

If you see these signs in the relationships currently taking up a large amount of your time and energy, it is probably time to make some changes and to set some clear boundaries. Keep in mind that this doesn't mean every relationship that is "surfacey" is also toxic and needs to be eliminated. There will always be a time when exchanging pleasantries and platitudes is perfectly normal and acceptable. Remember — it's not actually possible to cultivate a *real* relationship with everyone. We have to be choosey. Eliminating toxic and superficial relationships is not, for the most part, an all-or-nothing proposition. It doesn't mean simply picking a few friends to keep as your besties and then kicking the rest to the curb. On the contrary, it means cutting back on the time and energy you spend worrying about or investing in the relationships that don't matter all that much.

Here are a few examples of what setting these types of boundaries may look like:

1. **Cutting back on social media.** Facebook and other social media platforms have become such a pervasive part of our lives and daily habits that we hardly even think about it anymore. Most of us probably have no idea how much time we actually spend interacting online rather than in person, but suffice to say it is a lot. Enough that most of us feel lost without our smart phones by our side, and that we can't wait for more than a few seconds before needing to distract ourselves with the latest news feed. If you're not sure how much Facebook and social media are affecting your social life, why not try a little experiment? For the first week, keep a log of every time you visited Facebook, what you read there, and how it made you feel. Then, for the second week, stay off social media altogether. Delete the app from your phone and block the URL from your browser, but avoid publicly "announcing" your hiatus in a status update — let it be just for you. Every time you feel like logging on, send a text message to one of your close friends instead — and write down how that makes you feel. At the end of the two weeks, after comparing your results, you should have a pretty good idea of how much Facebook and social media are affecting you.

2. **Avoiding "frenemies."** We (women) are amazingly adept at surrounding ourselves with other women we call our friends but secretly don't really even like. These high-stress

competitions play out like a chess match between two masters, each one trying to outwit, outplay, and one-up the other, all under the guise of friendship. Why? Why do we do this to each other? And why do we let ourselves be sucked in to the game when we know it's a game we can't possibly win? It is possible to back away from a toxic "frenemy" relationship, but it means being willing to draw a firm line in the sand and just say no. Every. Single. Time. After all, the only way to win is not to play.

3. **Begin communicating your limits.** Some friends may be stepping on our toes simply because we haven't clearly communicated our boundaries or limits. For example, if a friend annoys you by consistently calling at an inconvenient time, have you ever told her so? When a relationship is consistently one-sided or draining, it is up to us to let our friends know, however gently, that we are setting a few boundaries for ourselves.

4. **Limiting exposure to other toxins.** While we should avoid certain relationships altogether, there are others that, for whatever reason, we can't completely eliminate from our lives. In those cases, sometimes the best we can do is simply limit the damaging exposure as much as possible. Once we've recognized the effect that a person has on us, whether it's causing us to feel insecure or angry, making us feel jealous or guilty, or even exposing us to excessive amounts of criticism, we can then begin to develop strategies for coping with those feelings. Sometimes it may mean speaking up for ourselves and saying, "Please don't speak to me that way; if you continue, I will leave." Sometimes it may simply mean making an excuse and cutting the visit short.

We may not be able to eliminate every toxic or superficial relationship in our lives, but we can certainly make great strides at eliminating *some* of them. And not only will cutting back on those damaged, dangerous, and destructive connections allow us more time and energy to cultivate those vitally important *real* relationships, but learning to be purposeful with the people in our lives right now will help set us up for even better relationships in the future.

Cultivating Depth

I don't think many of us aspire to be a mediocre friend. As a general rule, we don't usually set out to fill our lives with superficial, surface-level friends or to fill our address book with a long list of acquaintances. It just sort of happens. Life gets busy, filled up with activities and obligations, or we get burned once or twice by someone we let get too close. Those we were close to at one time drift away because they moved away or because we entered a different stage of life. We hang on to those superficial relationships because, in many ways, they are just easier. They don't threaten to break us. They are just what's there.

But what if we took the time to start cultivating *real* relationships in our lives? What if we refused to settle for mediocrity and instead took the time to nurture friendships that were real and honest and true? What if becoming unstuffed meant choosing quality over quantity in our personal lives, not just with the objects in our home? How would that change our outlook on life?

We've already talked about what a real relationship looks like, about the characteristics and qualities it imbues; likewise, we've also identified the red flags and warning signs of a superficial or toxic relationship. We know what we should be aiming for, as well as what we need to avoid. But how do we get there? How do we go about repairing fractured friendships or cultivating new ones? What's the first step?

One of the most important rules of friendship is also one of the most basic — in order to *have* a friend, you must *be* a friend. If you sit around waiting for friendships to cultivate on their own, without any effort on your part, you'll probably be waiting a very long time. It takes effort and intention to be a good friend, and to cultivate real relationships in your life. Here are a few practical ideas to help get you started.

1. **Take initiative.** There is no reason to sit around waiting for someone else to make the first move. If you've ever wondered why you don't have more authentic friendships in your life, have you ever stopped to consider the possibility that you might not be trying hard enough? When it comes right down to it, it's not that hard to reach out with a smile or a kind word — you just have to be conscious of it! The same goes for the friends you already have — you must nurture those friendships or they will go away. When was the last time you invited a friend over for coffee or even just gave them a quick call to see how they were doing? It takes very little effort to send out a quick text message every now and then. At the very least, start there.

2. **Be intentional.** A big part of taking the initiative to improve your relationships means taking the time to be intentional about who you are reaching out to. Who are the people in your life you would like to be pursuing a closer, deeper relationship with? This could be anyone from old friends you may have lost touch with to perhaps some newer acquaintances you've met recently whom you'd like to get to know better. Don't make your list too long — remember, this is about quality, not necessarily quantity.

3. **Prioritize face-to-face friendships.** Sometimes we can spend so much energy investing in old friends or acquaintances via Facebook or Instagram that we neglect real friendships we could make or deepen in real life right now. Make an effort to spend less time online and more time chatting with the people in your face-to-face world — other moms at your

child's school, friends from your Bible study or book club, and even neighbors you haven't spent much time with before.

4. **Listen.** So much of social media is about putting your own life on display, hoping to elicit a response. If you're not careful, that dynamic can spill over into real-life friendships too, where you go on and on about yourself in the hope of gaining the response you desire — admiration, encouragement, sympathy, or esteem. So turn this dynamic on its head. Instead of being so eager to share your own trials, tribulations, and triumphs, try focusing on the person you are connecting with. My husband always reminds me, "You have two ears and one mouth — use them accordingly." He's right.

5. **Pray.** Nothing changes the way we feel about someone or makes us care for them more deeply than praying for them regularly. If you don't already, begin including your friends on your daily prayer list. And if you're not sure what to ask for, just ask them. Take a minute or two to send them a quick text or email to find out what their needs are right now. While it might seem like nothing, this one small act can be completely transformative to your relationships.

6. **Go deep.** Be willing to talk about the hard stuff, both in your life and theirs. Don't allow your close friendships to slip into that fallback "everything's great and my life is perfect" mode we tend to hide behind. Be vulnerable. Let those who care about you know where you are struggling and what isn't so great in your life right now, and be willing to be a sounding board for their struggles as well.

7. **Make time for friendship.** Remember the most basic rule of friendship? In order to *have* a friend, you must *be* a friend. *Even when you are busy.* Cultivating real relationships in your life means becoming purposeful about making time for them and blocking out space in your schedule to devote to

the people who matter most in your life. It could be as simple as a regular phone call, a monthly lunch date, or an annual retreat just for the girls. It's not always about what you do, but that you make the effort and reserve the time to allow your friendships to flourish.

When it comes to the real relationships in your life, try not to waste your time on bitterness because you are feeling left out. Because as it turns out, that friend you think may have forgotten all about you is feeling just as busy, overwhelmed, or neglected as you are. The reality is that we all tend to get wrapped up in our own little worlds and forget to nurture our friendships the way we should. Even so, taking the time to reach out without expecting anything in return—taking the time to cultivate real relationships—is one of the most important things we will ever do.

When Our Friends Let Us Down

Of course, even when we take the time to nurture our friendships and cultivate real relationships, there will be times when a friendship goes awry. There is just something about female friendships that has the potential to send us right back to junior high! At thirty-seven, I'd like to think I am well past all that girl drama. I have many wonderful acquaintances, but only a very small handful of people I would consider to be my close friends, my "people."

Those are the ones I trust completely, the ones I can pour my heart out to, and the ones I know will be there for me no matter what—the ones immune to all the jealousy and pettiness and cattiness that so often crop up between us women. They are the ones for whom no explanation is necessary when we haven't talked for a while, the ones who can pick up exactly where we left off, like no time has passed. They are the ones who won't ever let me down.

Except, of course, when they do.

What then?

Not long ago, I found myself in exactly this situation. One of my closest friends was suddenly not so close anymore, and I had no idea what had gone wrong. For a while, I tried to blow it off, to brush away my gut feeling that something wasn't quite right. I even called to apologize for anything I may have done that had caused the rift I was feeling. She assured me that it was nothing, that she wasn't mad, that I hadn't done anything wrong — but still, the uneasiness lingered. I wondered if I might just be paranoid, but I could tell — something just wasn't right.

As time went on, it became more and more clear that I wasn't just being paranoid. Instead, this friend — the one I had trusted and leaned on, admired and looked up to, stayed up until all hours talking to, the one I would do anything for — was, for whatever reason, quite clearly no longer interested in my friendship. She stopped responding to emails and text messages and seemed to never have time to chat, even though I could see from her social media posts that she was making plenty of time for her other friends.

And then, in the moment I needed her most, she completely let me down. I had reached out to ask for help on a project that was very important to me. I sent her both a long email explaining what was going on and two text messages asking her to check her email and letting her know that the project was somewhat time sensitive. She ignored them all.

It crushed me.

All at once, I felt like I was fourteen years old again. I replayed every conversation, every email, every text message, over and over again in my head. I cried. Then I got angry. Then I cried some more. What had I *done*?

Finally, feeling completely lost, I did the only thing I knew to do — I called Edie to talk about it. As my accountability partner, she was sure to have some good advice, I told myself. If nothing else, she would be a shoulder to cry on. I half hoped she would commiserate with me and reassure me that this other friend was just a jerk, and that I would be perfectly justified to never speak to her again.

But that's not quite what happened.

She *did* commiserate, and while she understood why I was hurt and angry, her advice took me completely off guard.

"I think you should give her grace," she said quietly.

Every part of me protested. "But *she* is the one who should apologize! She is the one who hurt me! She doesn't *deserve* grace!"

"No, she doesn't," Edie agreed. "But neither do we."

Oh, right.

Chagrined and humbled, I promised to try to give her grace, even if I didn't feel like it. And wouldn't you know it? Not twenty-four hours later, an opportunity arose. The very same friend who had let me down now needed a favor from me.

Oh, friends, I had to dig deep on this one. The *last thing on earth* I felt like doing right at that moment was doing anything to help the friend who had just wounded me, particularly when she had not shown an ounce of remorse or spoken one word of apology.

But I did it anyway.

And you know what? It didn't fix our damaged friendship. There was no dramatic change of heart, no "aha" moment, no tearful reconciliation. Just the opposite, in fact. She never said thank you, or even recognized my contribution, and a short time later, she hurt me yet again. I have had to come to terms with the fact that our friendship will probably never again be what it once was.

But although it didn't fix anything, it did make me feel better. It took away the bitterness that was filling my heart and allowed me to let go of the hurt and anger I was feeling. It has also allowed me to have a lot more compassion and to accept the possibility that perhaps the problem isn't something I've done, but maybe just a result of something she is going through.

And while in this case I was on the receiving end of someone else's failure, I know there have been plenty of times when *I've* been the one who failed. I have lost relationships because I didn't come through in a pinch or because I let the connection wither and die. I've also committed my fair share of friendship felonies, from intentionally ignoring a request to missing a major event, or even worse. In those instances, sometimes I apologized and yet discovered it wasn't enough to warrant forgiveness, while other times, quite honestly, a relationship didn't mean enough to me to pursue or repair. I realized my mistake or my loss, mourned it internally, and moved on. But sometimes I admitted my failings to the friend I had let down, felt the hand of grace extended back to me, and was able to deepen a friendship with someone who saw me at my worst and yet loved, accepted, and forgave me anyway. Those are the friendships I treasure. Those are the ones I work hard to maintain.

Showing and Receiving Grace

It takes effort and intentionality to be a good friend and to cultivate real and meaningful relationships. It means being willing to put yourself out there and risk being hurt. And inevitably, there will be times when our friends disappoint us and let us down. They will hurt our feelings. They will annoy us. They will forget to show up or say something stupid or make a decision we don't agree with. They will be flawed, imperfect, and inadequate. In other words, they will be human. In the same way, we will hurt their feelings. We will annoy them. We will forget to show up or say something stupid. In other words, we will need to be forgiven.

To have a friend, we must be a friend, and ultimately that means showing grace when our friends don't come through the way we want them to and admitting our failings and accepting grace from our friends when we are the ones who flub up. It means forgiving and being forgiven, striving for the good in the midst of the bad, and treating our friends the way we'd like to be treated—the way God has already treated us.

Becoming unstuffed in our relationships doesn't mean throwing out some friends and keeping others. It's much more complicated than that. Instead, it is first recognizing the qualities of a *real* relationship, as well as being able to identify the signs of a toxic or superficial one. It means learning how to set boundaries so we can limit the amount of time and mental energy spent on relationships that don't matter in order to have more time to devote to those that do. It means cultivating those special friendships and showing grace when the people we love let us down, and admitting fault and receiving grace when *we've* let *them* down.

When it comes to relationships, let's not settle for mediocrity.

BASIC RULES OF REAL RELATIONSHIPS

Have you ever stopped to consider the fact that everyone has some unspoken rules for their friendships—and that the rules go two ways? The least fraught, longest lasting, and most rewarding friendships seem to balance both sides of the equation. Whenever one side is "off," the friendship will eventually and inevitably fall apart.

Reciprocity

I am okay if I interact with you X number of times a week/month/year. You are okay if you interact with me X number of times a week/month/year. We both want to keep in touch.

Remembrance

I am delighted if you remember X but will be okay if you forget. You are delighted if I remember X but are okay if I forget.

Reliability

I need you sometimes but will forgive you if you can't always come through. You need me sometimes but will forgive me if I can't always come through.

Rejoicing

I affirm and celebrate your successes. In turn, you affirm and celebrate my successes.

Respect

I recognize your boundaries and limits and strive to honor them. You recognize my boundaries and limits and strive to honor them.

Recognition

I recognize and affirm the value you add to my life. You recognize and affirm the value I add to your life. Or even deeper, I recognize your inherent value, flawed as you are, and love you. You recognize my inherent value, flawed as I am, and love me.

Refining

I am able to be honest with you to help you become a better person. You are able to be honest with me to help me become a better person.

Reward

Spending time with you is a pleasure and a joy. And spending time with me is a pleasure and a joy to you!

eight

Wellness

Finding Balance in a Chaotic World

What is joy without sorrow? What is success without failure? What is a win without a loss? What is health without illness? You have to experience each if you are to appreciate the other. There is always going to be suffering. It's how you look at your suffering, how you deal with it, that will define you.

Mark Twain

After nearly four straight years of too much stress, too little sleep, practically zero exercise, and way too much travel, my body had finally had enough. As much as I tried to keep pushing, to keep powering through despite how bad I felt, I couldn't stop getting sick. Over the course of one painfully long year, I battled the flu, two rounds of strep throat, bronchitis, walking pneumonia, an ear infection, and multiple urinary tract infections. In that time, I was prescribed antibiotics five different times and spent most of my waking hours coughing, blowing my nose, and generally just feeling miserable.

I was a mess.

And I had no one to blame except myself.

My body was telling me, in no uncertain terms, that it was all too much for me. And yet, I couldn't stop. Taking time off to be sick would only leave me further behind, and so I just kept powering through, waking up at the crack of dawn every single day to get more work done, then staying up late to spend time with my husband. I wanted to be everything to everyone — Super Mom, Super Wife, Super Blogger, Super Friend, Super Christian — despite the signs that were obvious to everyone but me.

Something had to give.

I wish I could point to some dramatic turning point that changed everything overnight, but balance and wellness don't really work that way. I finally just got sick and tired of being sick and tired all the time. And while it took me a really long time to even acknowledge the problem at all, it has also taken a very long time to begin to correct it, to cut out the unhealthy habits in my life in favor of incorporating healthy ones. It is a process I am still figuring out, and one I will probably have to work at for the rest of my life.

Again, it may seem a bit strange in a book about decluttering to talk about wellness and balance, and what that even means. But becoming unstuffed in the true sense of the word is about so much more than simply throwing things away. Our spirits have been littered with not only the rubble of superficial or toxic relationships but also with the strain of stressful, unhealthy, or even harmful behaviors, emotions, or situations.

Before we dive in, let me just state for the record that I am *by no means* an expert on health and wellness or stress management. I have no background in nutrition. I am not a sleep expert. I am not a doctor. Nor have I mastered the art of balance. I still struggle with working too much, sleeping too little, not taking time off, and trying to keep my own stress level under control. I don't eat as healthy as I could or as I know I should. All I can share is what I've learned along the way, as well as a little of what has worked for me.

In chapter 4, we began talking a little bit about balance and what that looks like in terms of our too-busy calendars and overbooked schedules. We discovered that while we often think balance is something we can *do*, balance actually happens when we *stop* doing and just rest. I think the importance of rest is an observation that bears frequent repeating, simply because it is so counterintuitive to our DIY, fix-it culture. It's certainly one I have to remind myself of regularly. We want to believe we can *create* balance.

But balance comes from rest.

Identifying Our Triggers

The seriously detrimental health effects from stress in our culture have practically reached epidemic proportions, to the point that, by some estimates, 75 to 90 percent of all doctor visits occur because of stress-related ailments.[17] High stress levels have been linked to a variety of serious physical problems, including heart disease, high blood pressure, stomach pains, asthma, hair loss, and even premature aging. Even scarier, too much stress actually alters the neurochemical makeup of your body and accounts for approximately 30 percent of all infertility problems. Left unchecked, too much stress can lead to migraines, depression, ulcers, heart attacks, and even strokes.

In other words, our stress is killing us.

And so while balance in our day-to-day lives may be passive, only happening once we are willing to stop doing and start resting, the act of eliminating the obvious stressors in our life must be active. Reducing our exposure to the things that cause stress is something that each of us can and should begin to work on. Our health depends on it.

Of course, that's easier said than done. Sometimes it feels like the things that are causing the most stress are out of our control. Other times it feels like the weight of the world is literally resting on our shoulders and could crush us at any moment. Sometimes we are so afraid of letting other people see us fail that we internalize what we perceive as everyone else's expectations. And then there are times when we find ourselves in a season of extreme stress, whether from a move, a job loss, a death, or some other major life event.

HOW STRESSED ARE YOU?

The Holmes and Rahe Stress Scale was developed in 1967 to determine your likelihood of developing an illness based on the amount of stress in your life. They identified forty-three major life events and gave each one a relative score based on the amount of stress it may cause. To determine your own likelihood for stress, assess the past two years and add up your total score based on the life events that apply to you.

100 Death of a spouse

73 Divorce

65 Major marital strife and/or separation

63 Imprisonment

63 Death of a close family member

53 Personal injury or illness

50 Marriage

47 Being fired or let go

45 Marriage reconciliation

45 Retirement

44 Change in health of a family member

40 Pregnancy

39 Sexual difficulties

39 Gaining a new family member

39 Business readjustment

38 Change in financial state

37 Death of a close friend

36 Change in jobs or occupation

35 Change in frequency of arguments

32 Major mortgage

30 Foreclosure of mortgage or loan

29 Change in responsibilities at work

29 Child leaving home

29	Trouble with in-laws
28	Outstanding personal achievement
26	Spouse starts or stops working
26	Beginning or ending school
25	Change in living conditions
24	Revision of personal habits
23	Trouble with boss
20	Change in working hours or conditions
20	Change in residence
20	Change in schools
19	Change in recreation
19	Change in church activities
18	Change in social activities
17	Minor mortgage or loan
16	Change in sleeping habits
15	Change in number of family get-togethers
15	Change in eating habits
13	Vacation
12	Major holiday
11	Minor violation of the law

Scoring:

Less than 150: slight risk of illness

150–299: moderate risk of illness

More than 300: high risk of illness

The fact is, the things that cause the greatest degree of stress will vary greatly from person to person and from season to season. Even so, they generally fall within one of the following categories:

- **Relationship stress.** This is the stress that gets attached to all the interpersonal interactions in our lives, whether they're with our spouses, parents, siblings, children, friends, or other acquaintances. This type of stress can be ongoing — a particular person we just can't get along with — or a onetime occurrence, such as a fight or a falling-out over political or religious beliefs. It ranges from the trivial — an annoying neighbor who won't leave you alone — to the devastating, such as a bitter divorce or a major falling-out with a family member.

- **Financial stress.** This is the stress that is connected to any sort of money issues, whether it's the strain of not having enough money to cover basic expenses; the chaos of not having a good handle on your finances, regardless of how much you have; or even the added pressure and responsibility that come from having an excess of money. While it would seem that having lots of money would alleviate stress, the fact is that sometimes more money just causes bigger problems. Financial stress also ranges from the minor — perhaps not being as organized as you'd like to be — to the major, such as bankruptcy or home foreclosure.

- **Work stress.** This is the stress that is associated with all things work-related, whether it comes from a job you hate, a demanding boss, a backstabbing coworker, irate customers, unreasonable sales goals, long work hours, or simply a high-pressure deadline. Work stress isn't necessarily limited to a job or workplace you hate; even a job you truly love can come with a fair amount of stress.

- **Health stress.** This is the stress that comes from illness and health problems. It ranges from minor issues such as general fatigue, an injury, or a weakened immune system to major issues like chronic illness or pain, a disability, or cancer. Health stress is certainly not limited to your own health issues; it can also come from having a close family member or friend struggling with these health issues.

- **Emotional stress.** This is the stress that comes from a trauma or severe emotional blow — betrayal, abuse, an accident or catastrophe, as well as guilt over something we did (or didn't do). It can involve extreme feelings of sadness, remorse, loneliness, grief, fear, anxiety, or even depression.

- **Physical stress.** This is the stress that comes from activities that are physically taxing or exhausting, such as travel, physical labor, long work hours, and the care of babies. Lack of sleep or exercise contributes to physical stress, as do poor eating habits and addictions to tobacco, alcohol, or drugs.

- **Spiritual stress.** This may be one of the most overlooked sources of stress, but this type of stress can appear in both those who consider themselves religious and those who don't. For Christians living in an increasingly secular culture in which traditional beliefs often run counter to political correctness, this stress can manifest itself as shame, guilt (real or false), selfishness, rebellion, or even distancing oneself from God and living out of sync with the way the Bible says we should live. However, for those without religious affiliations, this type of stress can manifest itself as feelings of hopelessness or despair, or in feeling a lack of purpose in life.

BIBLICAL WISDOM ON STRESS AND REST

The Bible has a lot to say about dealing with stress and the importance of rest. If you need a reminder, consider the following verses:

On Stress

Yet you desired faithfulness even in the womb; you taught me wisdom in that secret place (Psalm 51:6).

Wash away all my iniquity and cleanse me from my sin (Psalm 51:3).

Fear and trembling have beset me; horror has overwhelmed me. I said, "Oh, that I had the wings of a dove! I would fly away and be at rest. I would flee far away and stay in the desert; I would hurry to my place of shelter, far from the tempest and storm" (Psalm 55:5–8).

Cast your cares on the LORD and he will sustain you; he will never let the righteous be shaken (Psalm 55:22).

Have mercy on me, my God, have mercy on me, for in you I take refuge. I will take refuge in the shadow of your wings until the disaster has passed (Psalm 57:1).

Do you not know that your bodies are temples of the Holy Spirit, who is in you, whom you have received from God? You are not your own; you were bought at a price. Therefore honor God with your bodies (1 Corinthians 6:19–20).

On Rest

I lie down and sleep; I wake again, because the LORD sustains me (Psalm 3:5).

In peace I will lie down and sleep, for you alone, LORD, make me dwell in safety (Psalm 4:8).

The LORD is my shepherd, I lack nothing. He makes me lie down in green pastures, he leads me beside quiet waters, he refreshes my soul (Psalm 23:1–3).

In vain you rise early and stay up late, toiling for food to eat—for [God] grants sleep to those he loves (Psalm 127:2).

When you lie down, you will not be afraid; when you lie down, your sleep will be sweet (Proverbs 3:24).

[Jesus said,] "Come to me, all you who are weary and burdened, and I will give you rest" (Matthew 11:28).

Regardless of where the stress comes from, the effects on our overall well-being are often the same. Stress chips away at our psyches, making us feel helpless and despondent, or angry and bitter. It eats away at our health, contributing to physical pain, problems sleeping, weight gain, and much more. Even so, only after we have begun to identify where our stress is coming from can we start to look for a solution.

So what do we do?

Small, Purposeful Changes

Of course naming and identifying our stressors is only the *first* step in attempting to unstuff our lives from the weight of excess stress; we still have to develop solutions for coping with chronic stress or find a way to eliminate certain stressors altogether. In the midst of a stressful situation, it can seem really difficult—if not impossible—to see any sort of solution. But believe it or not, just a few small tweaks in our day-to-day lives can put the stress that seems so big and unmanageable back into perspective.

The reality is that stress can often become a vicious cycle of cause and effect—we feel stressed about one thing, which causes us to sleep less, stop exercising, or work nonstop, which in turn compounds our stress even more. The more stressed we feel, the more it affects everything else around us. The only way to reduce the stress—or eliminate it altogether—is to make conscious healthy choices, even when we don't really feel like it.

In my own life, I discovered this firsthand. My struggles with constantly getting sick were the physical manifestation of all the stress I had been dealing with for years—and not just stress I had created for myself through starting my own business. On the Holmes and Rahe Stress Scale—a test developed by two psychologists to measure the amount of stress in your life, as well as your likelihood of getting sick as a result—my stress level was practically off the charts. Over the span of just a few years, we had changed jobs; moved cross-country; had a high-needs, colicky baby; renovated our house; dealt with the chronic illness of one close family member and the cancer of another; and eventually mourned the death of both. These were big life events, many outside of my immediate control, but they all added up, and the result was chronic exhaustion and a weakened immune system.

And while there were lots of factors outside of my control that I knew I couldn't do anything about, I also knew that something had to give. I realized that the only option was to focus on those things I could do, the small changes I could make instead of trying to worry so much about the things that felt out of control. So I began making small but purposeful changes in my daily habits—changes I knew might not remove the stress itself but would certainly help alleviate the symptoms.

The reality of life is that there will always be stressful circumstances and situations that are outside of our control. If you take a look at the Holmes and Rahe chart on pages 182–83, you'll see that many of life's stressors are not necessarily bad things—such as a new marriage, the birth of a child, a new job, or a new home—and most of the others are things that simply happen to us, regardless of how hard we may try to prevent them. Our only option, really, for the sake of our own sanity, is to develop coping mechanisms and habits that focus on the areas within our control so we are equipped to better handle the unavoidable stress that comes our way.

In my own battle to combat stress, there are three distinct areas I have tried to focus on — sleep, exercise, and downtime. Each has had a profound impact on improving my health, healing my immune system, and keeping my stress level down.

Sleep

I don't think there is any one factor that can contribute more to stress than a *lack* of sleep, and no one solution that can help alleviate stress more than a good night's sleep. Many of us — especially those of us under a lot of stress — are chronically sleep deprived. There aren't enough hours in the day to get it all done, so we chip away at our resting hours, staying up too late, getting up too early, and never allowing ourselves a full night of sleep. According to a recent survey by the Better Sleep Council, 53 percent of adult women regularly don't allow themselves to get the recommended seven to eight hours of sleep per night.[18] In fact, according to a recent Gallup poll, the average amount of sleep for American adults as a whole is only 6.8 hours per night.[19]

Lack of sleep and chronic exhaustion, like excess stress, are related to a whole host of problems, ranging from poor work performance and driving accidents to relationship issues and mood disorders like excessive anger or depression. It also contributes to health risks, including heart disease, diabetes, and obesity. Chronic sleep loss has even been linked to early death.[20] Clearly, this is not something we want to mess around with.

While the effects of sleep loss are sobering and scary, the solution is pretty simple: Get more sleep.

Of course, simple doesn't always mean easy, and for some of us — especially those of us who have gone for a long time on less sleep than we should—it will mean working hard, at least at first, to make more sleep a priority. Luckily there are some very practical and easy-to-implement steps that can help us get a better night's sleep.

1. **Be consistent.** Going to bed and waking up at the same time each day—even on the weekends and holidays—help our bodies reinforce a regular sleep-wake cycle. Eventually our bodies will just "know" when it is time to go to bed, which makes it much easier to fall asleep. Our bodies will also know when it is time to rise—often before our alarm even goes off—allowing us to wake up completely refreshed.

2. **Avoid screen time before bed.** Multiple studies have shown that backlit screens from television, computers, tablets, and even our phones can dramatically impact our sleep. The light coming from the screen artificially alters our sleepiness level and suppresses our melatonin levels, which in turn makes it harder to fall asleep and reduces the quality of the sleep we do get. Moreover, even seemingly innocuous activities such as watching television or checking email before bed can impact our sleep, not just from the backlighting but from the stimulation of the content itself. Our brains will continue processing what we've seen or read even after we turn it off, and these thoughts can make it difficult to settle down and actually get to sleep.

3. **Create a bedtime ritual.** Establishing a simple routine before bed is an effective way to let your brain and body know it is time to wind down. This could be as simple as brushing your teeth and putting on your pajamas, but if getting enough sleep has been a problem, you might need to put a little more effort into your ritual—drinking a cup of herbal tea, reading a (nonelectronic) book for fifteen or twenty minutes, or even doing some light stretches. My own bedtime routine consists of drinking a glass of Natural Calm (a magnesium supplement) and then applying some calming essential oils to my feet and

pulse points. (I use lavender, chamomile, cedarwood, and a blend by Young Living called Peace & Calming.) The entire ritual takes only a few minutes, but it is enough to get my brain and body ready for sleep, no matter how wound up I might be.[*]

4. **Avoid caffeine after noon.** Having grown up in the Pacific Northwest, where the unconditional love of java is completely ingrained into our psyches almost from birth, I could literally drink coffee morning, noon, and night. I can't get enough of the stuff. Unfortunately, that love of all things caffein-ated has some serious drawbacks, the biggest of which is its effect on sleep. Similar to the effect of backlit screens, too much caffeine disrupts our sleep by shortening our deep sleep time and causing us to wake up more frequently. Even small quantities of caffeine can affect sleep, and a 2012 study found that caffeine consumed up to six hours before bed has the biggest detrimental impact.[21] Thus, avoiding any sort of caffeinated beverages after lunchtime can have a big impact on the overall quality of your sleep.

5. **Keep a record.** It's easy to justify or rationalize our lack of sleep if we're not fully paying attention. We can even tell ourselves it's not that bad or fool ourselves into thinking we are getting more sleep than we really are. The only way to actually know whether we are getting enough sleep on a regular basis is to keep track of it. Luckily, technology has made this very easy! There are a variety of fitness bands and smart phone apps currently on the market that will help you track your sleep. For the past year, I have been using an iPhone app called Sleep Cycle, which not only tracks my sleep each night but also wakes me up during my lightest sleep cycle within a given time frame, which makes it far easier

---

[*] For instructions on how to get more details about my sleep routine, see page 219 at the back of the book.

to get up in the morning! It has been both fascinating and motivating to watch my sleep habits improve over time.

6. **Find accountability.** If you don't sleep alone, it is essential to have your spouse on board with, or at least supportive of, your attempts to get more sleep. Having a cheerleader and someone to hold you accountable when necessary can make all the difference in the world. Just last night, for instance, I had planned to go to bed early in order to get up early this morning and write. However, when I got into bed, what I really wanted to do was watch the next episode of my latest Netflix obsession. The second I turned on the TV, my husband (whom I had asked just that morning to make sure I went to bed on time) walked into the room and demanded to know what I was doing. He insisted I turn off the TV immediately and then proceeded to turn off the light and close the bedroom door so I could get to sleep. Within minutes, I was out. Even better? I was able to get a ton of work done this morning, all thanks to him! Accountability works.

If you are going to make only *one* change in your life as a result of this book, let it be getting more sleep. A well-rested brain is not only happier, healthier, and more productive; it is better equipped to handle stress, regardless of where the stress comes from. Sleep changes our perspective. It makes problems that felt insurmountable seem manageable. It is the magic bullet and the miracle cure to excess stress. And it is the one thing you can do right now that may just make all the difference in the world.

Movement and Exercise

While improving our sleep habits is probably the biggest single change any of us can make to reduce stress in our day-to-day lives, the amount of movement and exercise we get plays a very big role as well. The truth is that modern life has made it far too easy for most of us to become almost completely sedentary. We spend the day sitting at a desk, tied to our computer screens, and then we come home and veg out in front of the TV, needing downtime to decompress from the stress of the day. Don't believe me? Consider that the average American spends 9.3 hours sitting each day, which, if you are paying attention, is almost an hour and a half *more* than we spend sleeping.

This lack of movement not only compounds our stress levels, but it is downright dangerous to our health as well. Women who sit for more than six hours per day are 40 percent likelier to die within the next fifteen years than women who sit less than three hours per day.[22] Furthermore, people who hold "sitting" jobs are twice as likely to suffer from cardiovascular disease. According to a recent article in *Bloomberg Businessweek*, "When you sit, the muscles are relaxed, and enzyme activity drops by 90% to 95%, leaving fat to camp out in the bloodstream. Within a couple hours of sitting, healthy cholesterol plummets by 20%."[23]

Like our lack of sleep problem, the solution to this sitting epidemic is pretty simple — we need to get moving. Even so, that task is often easier noted than done, especially when we don't always have control over our working environment. Even so, the following list includes a few practical changes that anyone can make, regardless of whether you are working full-time or don't move enough at home.

1. **Use a pedometer.** As with sleep, it's easy to convince ourselves we are doing much better than we really are when it comes to getting enough movement and exercise during the day. However, when we start actually keeping track of the number of steps we take, there can be no doubt as to whether we are moving enough. It is frequently recommended that we aim to walk at least ten thousand steps per day, which for the average walker is the equivalent of about five miles. While that number is only a common recommendation and not a hard-and-fast rule, chances are, for those of us who spend our

day sitting, we are not getting anywhere close to that number. Using a pedometer is the simplest way to find out.

2. **Work standing up.** Stand-up desks have become more and more common. Even if you work in a traditional office setting, you can purchase an adjustable standing desk attachment that allows you to both stand and sit right at your existing desk. About a year ago, I invested in a treadmill desk that allows me to walk and work at the same time. I have found that as long as I keep my speed low, I can work and write just as well — sometimes even better — as I can sitting down.

3. **Use a balance ball.** If a standing desk is not an option, consider swapping out your office chair for a Swiss balance or stability ball. These can be purchased at a sporting goods store for less than $30, and unlike a regular chair, a stability ball forces us to use more of our core muscles to stay balanced. It's still probably not as good as standing up or walking, but it is at least an improvement.

4. **Take frequent stretch breaks.** Whenever you have to sit for long periods of time, whether it's at work, on an airplane, or even at home, keep your body active by getting up to stretch at least once every ninety minutes. The easiest way to remember to do this is to set the timer on your phone. When it goes off, you get up, stretch out for a few minutes, and reset the timer for another ninety minutes.

5. **Go for a walk (or a bike ride).** The easiest way to incorporate more steps and movement into your day is to simply go for a walk. Make it a habit, whether it's a brisk twenty minutes in the morning, a relaxing walk with your spouse and kids after dinner, or a quick walk around the block during your lunch break. The more you make it a part of your regular routine, the easier it will be. If possible, you might walk or bike to work. Last year, my husband bought me an adult tricycle

for my birthday so I could ride it to work. I'm not really a big exercise person, so I wasn't expecting to love it, but the short ride home down our little town's scenic bike paths has easily become my favorite fifteen minutes of the day. It hasn't disrupted my routine; instead, it has improved it immensely.

I think sometimes we feel we have to make these huge changes to our exercise routine in order to make them count. If we're not running five miles a day or conquering the latest P90X workout video, why even bother? But when it comes to movement and exercise, just a few small tweaks in our daily routine can make a big difference for both our physical and mental health.

Downtime

The third area I've tried to focus on in this battle against stress and fatigue has to do with adding more downtime. In other words, I've had to work at simply learning how to rest and do nothing. For some people, this may be more difficult than for others, but I think for many of us, when there is always so much to do and not enough time to get it done, allowing ourselves real downtime — unstructured, unscheduled time in our day to simply relax — can actually be really difficult. After all, as we discussed in chapter 4, we live in a busy world that is constantly calling us to *do* something.

Just look at the way we structure our days. I don't know about you, but from the moment my alarm goes off in the morning, I am busy. Checking my email while I go to the bathroom and brush my teeth. Issuing a practice spelling test during breakfast. Juggling half a dozen projects, commitments, and obligations throughout the day. Skipping lunch to get more work done. Scrambling to make dinner and then help the kids finish their homework so we can all fall into bed completely exhausted and ready to wake up early and do it again the next day.

For me, this learning to just *chill out* sometimes has been the most challenging of all three areas, which is exactly why I need to keep reminding myself of how important it is. After all, I can see the benefits of getting more sleep, and I know adding more movement and exercise to my life is also necessary, but doing *nothing*? Really? How does that help anything? How does that make life better? Won't I feel more stressed if I'm not constantly working to improve my lot?

Surprisingly, the answer is no.

A recent article in the *New York Times* touted the benefits of relaxing, asserting the claim that, although it seems counterintuitive, taking more downtime actually makes us *more* productive, not less. The article pointed to a number of studies that have shown how power naps during the day can significantly improve memory and job performance and how employees who took longer vacations generally rated higher in their performance reviews. Furthermore, additional research by Professor K. Anders Ericsson at Florida State University has shown that our brains are designed to work most productively in ninety-minute intervals. When we attempt to override the signals of fatigue that our body sends, we end up causing more stress but not actually accomplishing any more work.[24]

So how *do* we learn to relax, especially if we're not really wired that way? How do we make more room for downtime when we've conditioned ourselves to be constantly on the go? Honestly this is one area I'm still working on, but I have found the following strategies to be helpful:

1. **Keep your weekends free.** In my little town of Punta Gorda, Florida, there is something happening almost every weekend, whether it's a music festival, art fair, or some other special event. In fact, the cultural opportunities are one of the things we loved about this town when we first moved here. But then we had kids, and with kids came even more activities and birthday parties and sporting events, and we got to a point where it felt like we never stopped running from one thing to the next. But then one day, we just finally decided that enough was enough. We stopped worrying about trying

to keep up and instead just decided to stay home. And you know what? We discovered that staying home is actually pretty great. While we still go out on occasion, we have now made a much bigger effort to keep our weekend plans as unscheduled as possible. We often stay in our pajamas all day, playing endless rounds of Skip-Bo or losing ourselves in a favorite book. The girls play; my husband and I talk; and we all end the weekend feeling refreshed and rejuvenated instead of exhausted. The simple act of planning to do nothing has made all the difference in the world.

2. **Let Go of the FOMO.** Fear Of Missing Out is a very real phenomenon in today's society. Over the years, I have lost count of the number of friends who seem to spend their entire life — every single evening and every single weekend — shuttling their kids from one activity to the next. They are caught in a trap of not wanting their kids to miss out on a single opportunity, but they don't seem to realize they are denying both themselves and their kids the joy and beauty of simply doing nothing. A vitally important part of childhood is learning how to entertain yourself, using your imagination, and building life skills through creative play. The simple fact is that the more we commit to, the less downtime we will have. As a family, it is important to let go of that fear of missing out and instead purposefully set limits on the number of activities you will commit to. Otherwise, the constant activity can very quickly and easily take over your whole life.

3. **Give yourself grace.** Somewhere along the way, especially since the advent of social media, where each of us now has an opportunity to share the most heavily edited versions of ourselves, we have deluded ourselves into thinking that every moment of every day needs to be *precious* and special. There is this unreasonable expectation that as parents, we are supposed to be fully engaged with our kids at all times, and

if we're not, we are failing. But what if we decided to lower our expectations just a tad and instead give ourselves a lot more grace? What if we decided to recognize that not every moment needs to be structured or Pinterest-worthy? What if, sometimes, we decided to just be okay with good enough?

Finding balance in a chaotic world is not always about eliminating stress completely, but sometimes about adjusting the way we handle it. After all, no matter how hard we work to eliminate stressors in our lives, there will always be some major stress points we can't do anything to change. Our only option, then, is to find better ways of coping with the stress that does come our way. In my own life, I've seen firsthand what a difference these small but purposeful changes can make. After fighting one illness after another, I was finally able to heal my immune system and stop getting sick. In fact, it has been almost a year since my last cold or illness, despite the fact that I have worked just as hard, taken on more responsibilities and projects, and traveled even more. By focusing on the small things I *could* do—getting more sleep, adding more movement and exercise to my day, and purposefully adding downtime to just relax—I have become much better equipped to deal with the big things I *can't* control. I don't know if I've achieved balance, but I am learning how to rest. And for now, that is good enough for me.

THE BENEFITS OF GOING TO CHURCH

A number of scientific studies have proven the incredible health and wellness benefits of going to church. It appears that those who attend religious services regularly have a significantly lower risk of depression, better time and life management skills, better grades, a longer life expectancy, and even better sex lives than their nonchurchgoing counterparts.[25]

It makes sense when you think about it. After all, church is social, and we are social creatures. We crave interaction and connection with other human beings, and we long for a place to belong, a community of people who care about us and accept us just as we are. Church fills that need. Church also usually involves prayer, quiet meditation, and music, all of which can help a person feel more relaxed and bring his or her blood pressure down. Furthermore, church provides us with a place to serve, and service has proven again and again to be good for us.[26]

But what is it about church that makes it better for us than attending, say, a book club, yoga class, or cultural or sporting event? As it turns out, church provides much that the secular world doesn't understand or even see:

- Church gives us a place to "unstuff" ourselves internally. In church, we confess and repent of the bad stuff we have done, and we receive unconditional grace and forgiveness from God.

- Church reminds us on a regular basis that we were created by and are loved by Someone more powerful and gracious than we could ever fathom.

- Church gives us a physical place to worship and draw near to God, to feel his power, and to focus on our relationship with him.

- Church gives us a place to receive the sacraments, a physical manifestation of the spiritual nourishment God provides.

- Church gives us a place to recognize other human beings as beloved children of God and to learn how to extend the grace and forgiveness we've been given to those around us.

nine

Spirit

Letting Go of the Need to Do It Yourself

To be convinced in our hearts that we have forgiveness of sins and peace with God by grace alone is the hardest thing.

Martin Luther

It was years ago, but I can still remember the sick feeling in my stomach like it was yesterday. The minute I stepped into their bedroom — which I had just meticulously cleaned in preparation for my oldest daughter Maggie's fourth birthday party — I felt ill. This was, of course, long before the great toy purge of 2011 that redefined our family and forever changed the way I looked at stuff. And in this particular moment, every single toy my children owned was strewn about the floor — an unidentifiable jumble of Legos, building blocks, play kitchen food, dress-up clothes, Barbies, Littlest Pet Shops, My Little Ponies, and all the four thousand accessories that are now mandatory for every toy sold. All the neatly labeled baskets full of clothes and accessories had been upended and tossed about. Crushed goldfish cracker crumbs mixed with spilled apple juice to create a sticky paste on the carpet, and what had once been a closet full of adorable clothing organized by size and color was just a pile on the floor. And to add insult to injury, I was pretty sure I smelled the unmistakable scent of pee.

How could eight small four-year-olds make such a mess in such a short amount of time? The damage done by Hurricane Charley paled in comparison to what these little tornadoes had done. How would I ever clean it up? Where would I even begin? I held back the urge to scream and then naturally did what any mom about to completely lose it would do: I closed the door and went back to the party that was still happening outside and pretended like absolutely nothing was wrong.

The Messes We Make

Do you ever feel like you've already made such a mess of things that at this point you couldn't possibly turn it around? Maybe you've shopped your way into a house so full of stuff that it is bursting at the seams. Maybe you've accumulated massive debt or perhaps even filed for bankruptcy. Perhaps out of boredom or desperation you've fallen into the trap of always needing the newest and best, overspending on things you really don't need to impress people who really don't matter. Maybe you've overcommitted yourself with too many activities and obligations, and you feel like you are running on a treadmill with no idea how to get off.

On the other hand, perhaps your mess is one others can't easily see or haven't noticed—one of deep depression or childhood trauma, wrapping you in a darkness you can't let go of or shrouding you in bitterness and anger over a wrong that was done to you. Perhaps it has been a secret double life tainted by alcohol abuse, drug use, or adultery. Or maybe it is less overtly sinister and more subtle—a house that never gets clean, bills consistently paid late, too much to do and too little time to get it done, and never feeling able to devote enough time or energy to the things or people you care about.

We all have our own messes.

Let me tell you a little about mine.

My big mess started sometime midway through my senior year

of college. Until that point, I had been a high achiever—a straight-A honors student, balancing a full-time job with a heavy course load. Eager to prove how grown up I was, I had married young, between my sophomore and junior year, and then, unwilling to face the cracks already forming in my marriage, volunteered to take in my two younger brothers. Perhaps I thought that by saving them I could save myself.

It didn't work.

In fact, in hindsight, it was the perfect storm. The flashbacks and nightmares of childhood sexual abuse that kept me up all night. The deepening sense of despair and hopelessness. The feeling that I was trapped in a marriage I knew had been a mistake from the beginning. The theology class that seemed to indicate religion was nothing more than different groups of men deciding what to believe at any given point in time. The philosophy class that made me question whether there was really any meaning to life at all. The pressure of needing to complete twenty-seven more credit hours in one semester to be able to graduate.

And then I got angry. A God who was real wouldn't have let those terrible things happen to me. A God who was real wouldn't have turned his back on me.

I decided to call BS.

This religion stuff was obviously a crock.

Thanks, but no thanks.

Of course, in the absence of God, life really did lose all meaning. If the God I had believed in so wholeheartedly my entire life suddenly ceased to exist, what then? What was the point? Why even bother?

And so I decided I wanted out.

Of all of it.

In the absence of meaning, suicide seemed like the logical choice.

Thus began a painfully long, two-and-a-half-year journey through a darkness and depression I wouldn't wish on my worst enemy. Six different psychiatric hospitals, countless doctors, therapists, and medications, an endless array of treatment plans and strategies and a myriad of really bad, self-destructive, and downright dangerous life choices in between hospital stays. And then, in an act of pure desperation for a cure, even electroshock therapy. Five suicide attempts, the worst of which, after the fire department broke down my door and restarted my heart in the ambulance, landed me in a coma on life support, with less than a 10 percent chance of ever waking up. My very survival was a miracle, and I was too depressed to even see it. By the time I hit rock-bottom, two and a half years after my first suicide attempt, I was divorced, bankrupt, and completely alone.

And then something *finally* clicked.

Not in a day, or even a month, but slowly the dark cloud of depression that had been hanging over me for so long began to lift. I started to think about living again, instead of planning for a way to die.

Thus began a new journey, one of trying to save myself. It was hard at first, awkward and strange. I got a job and decided to finish my degree so I could finally go to law school. But law school didn't seem quite ambitious enough all on its own, so I decided to apply to business school at the same time. I would do a dual-degree program and emerge with both a JD and MBA in only four years' time.

Well. As it turns out, I hated law school. And so I quit.

My next self-salvation project was a new marriage, quickly followed by a new baby. Having failed so badly on my first go-round, I was determined to make this marriage a success. I resolved to be the perfect wife, the perfect mom, the perfect homemaker, always wondering why I could never quite achieve the fulfillment I craved. My husband and I made a lot of changes in that time, always looking for that thing, that place, that job that would fulfill us. It wasn't that we were unhappy — we were financially secure, usually had plenty of friends wherever we went, and no shortage of nice things and fun activities to fill our time. In 2009, we added another beautiful little girl to our family, rounding our number to four. We had everything I thought I had ever wanted, and to all outside appearances, our life seemed perfect.

But something was still missing.

In the fall of 2009, just a few months after our second daughter was born, Chuck and I made the decision to move from Seattle back to Florida. It had become clear that my mother-in-law was no longer able to live on her own, so we made plans to pick her up in Chicago and take her to Florida to live with us. I wasn't eager to leave our comfortable little life in Seattle. The transition back to Punta Gorda was more than a little painful. The combination of caring for two small children and an octogenarian was trying on the best days and sheer misery on the worst. Our colicky six-month-old daughter kept us up for hours every night, usually crying nonstop from about 2:00 a.m. to 5:00 a.m. My mother-in-law had a whole other set of issues to manage — countless pills and endless doctor appointments, hearing and vision loss, high blood pressure, and difficulty keeping her balance. It often felt like we had three kids instead of two, and we were totally overwhelmed.

The few friends we did have nearby were either childless or long past the baby stage. Most simply couldn't relate to our stage of life, and they quickly dropped off the map, one by one. As the months went by, my despair grew. I was sleep deprived, lonely, bored, and miserable. I spent a lot of time feeling sorry for myself, and the rest of the time being angry with my husband for dragging me back to Florida.

Naturally, it was in *this* environment that we decided to remodel our home. Looking back, it's obvious the timing couldn't have been worse, but in the midst of our sleep-deprived misery, we both thought taking on the project we had dreamed about for almost five years would give us a new focus and make things better. Not surprisingly, it didn't.

I began shopping more and more. The more I shopped, the emptier and more miserable I felt, so to make up for it, I shopped even more. Chuck, understandably, responded to my out-of-control shopping habit with anger and frustration. That spring, our marriage — and our lives in general — were at a breaking point, and yet neither of us had a clue how to fix it, how to break the vicious cycle, or how to improve our situation. Once again, it felt like there was no way out.

Salvation came in the most unlikely form.

Long before my children were born, long before I was even born, long before Chuck and his sister, Linda, were grown, my mother-in-law, Marie, had dreamed that the train of her wedding dress would be made into a christening gown for her grandchildren. But life doesn't always turn out the way we expect. Linda opted not to have children, and when Chuck entered his forties still a bachelor, marriage or children seemed unlikely. By her eightieth birthday, Marie had given up hope of ever becoming a grandmother. When our first child was born, the christening gown—this lifelong dream of Marie's—became a hot topic of conversation. With Marie now eighty-three years old, we couldn't pass up the opportunity to have the dress made, but obviously we couldn't just put our daughter in the dress and not actually have her christened.

By that point, God and I had reached an understanding—or at least I thought we had. I would try to be a good person, and he would leave us alone. I was no longer angry with him, but I certainly wasn't interested in a relationship.

But baptism is a *big deal* to church people. They won't let you just walk in off the street and have your kid baptized. You have to be a *member* of the church. For Maggie's christening, we lucked out. I was technically still a member of the church I had grown up in, even though I hadn't attended services in at least ten years. Linda had the very special dress made, and Maggie was baptized the day after her first birthday in my hometown in Washington State. But as our second child Annie's first birthday approached, the pressure was mounting to also have her christened in "The Dress." We needed to find a nearby church—and fast.

And thus we began attending services at the closest church we could find, for the sole purpose of having our youngest daughter baptized. And although our motives for joining the church were far from honorable, we were surprised to discover we didn't hate it. The people there were so *nice*, going out of their way to talk to us and make us feel welcome. After having felt so isolated for so long, it was refreshing. Despite our reluctance, we kept going back, Sunday after Sunday. Eventually, we were invited to join a small group—a Bible study group—that met twice a month, an invitation we politely but firmly declined. After all, we were *barely* church people; we were definitely *not* Bible study kind of people!

It took a whole year of almost weekly invitations before we finally agreed to attend the small group, and it was still months and months after that before we actually looked forward to going. Every other week, Chuck and I would ponder how we might be able to get out of it without hurting anyone's feelings. We could never come up with a good excuse, and they were all just so nice, so we kept going.

God was working on me from all sides, nudging me, wearing me down, and pulling me closer in spite of my reluctance. Finally, one Sunday, after so many years of doing it on my own, I just stopped trying to resist.

I gave in and prayed, literally for the first time in many, many years: *"I can't do this on my own, Lord. I've tried, and I've failed. You want me? You can have me. I'm far from perfect, and I've made too many mistakes to count, but YOUR will be done."*

The peace I felt in that moment was overwhelming. Giving up control is a little scary, especially for a girl who *really* likes to be in control.

But in that moment, it all became so clear. All these events in my life, all these things that had, up until that point, seemed random and unrelated, now made sense. It was like I had been standing right in front of a giant tapestry, staring so closely at one small section that I couldn't see the larger picture. God pulled me back so I could see the whole thing, and it was far, far more beautiful than I could've ever imagined.

The emptiness was finally filled.

Every single step of the way, even when I had rejected and turned my back on God, even when I thought I could do it all on my own and save myself, even as I made one bad decision after another — he was there. Despite all my mistakes, all my stubbornness, all my insistence on doing it my way, God was there, protecting me, watching over me, *saving my life*, not once but *five times*, when by all accounts I should have died. He always, *always* placed the right people in the right place at the right time, all doing their part to bring me back to him.

Amazing grace — even for a train wreck like me.

Our Need to Achieve

My temptation, when I tell that story, is to just leave it there. All tied up with a neat little bow. Girl messes up. Girl finds God. Girl gets saved. Girl lives happily ever after. Cue the credits and touching theme song. Inspiring, right?

We all want the Hollywood ending.

But that wasn't the end.

Oh, don't get me wrong, I'm still saved by grace. That won't change.

But that mountaintop moment of peace and clarity, when all was suddenly right with the world? That didn't last forever. I am, for the most part, still a giant mess. (Though some days I hide it better than others.)

I think one of the biggest problems we face is this idea that once we have been saved, once we've triumphed over adversity and come out on the other side, we are somehow "fixed." It goes hand-in-hand with the belief that we, as Christians, are more or less supposed to be perfect, that we have to do the right things and say the right things and be the right things in order to count, and especially in order to maintain our salvation. I don't think the church necessarily *intends* to perpetuate this belief, but it comes through in almost everything we do. We are supposed to talk a certain way and dress a certain way and act a certain way. If we don't, then, well, clearly we just don't love Jesus enough. Or maybe we're not even really saved.

208

The problem with this belief is that it allows us to convince ourselves that our salvation depends on us. Yes, we may have screwed up or made a mess of things in the past, but now that we are saved, we should be better. It's time for our Hollywood ending. And if we're not better, we need to try harder. Do more. Get back to that mountaintop one more time. We focus on our need to achieve perfection and forget that the hard work has already been done for us, in spite of us. And when we inevitably mess up or lose our way or when others let us down, we are devastated, confused, and shaken to the core.

Last year, Chuck and I, along with a few other families, ended up leaving our church — yes, the very church that had brought us back to God — after a major falling-out with some of the leadership, those very same people who had first invited us in. It was a devastating, gut-wrenching breakup, and the months that followed were some of the darkest I have experienced since that horrible depression in my early twenties. In one fell swoop, we lost the community that had meant everything to us. For months, I couldn't bear the thought of going to church at all — it was simply too painful. Every time Chuck suggested we try someplace new, I would panic, paralyzed with fear at the thought of being hurt again. In fact, even now, more than a year later, we are still struggling to find a new church home. There is no neat bow, no happy ending to this story. It's still messy and ugly and hard.

But in the midst of this struggle, I have never been more acutely aware of my own need for grace, nor more comforted by the realization that God uses our imperfection to do his best work. In fact, if there is one thing the Bible makes abundantly clear again and again, it is that God uses the most messed-up, flawed, not-good-enough people to do his will again and again, because messed-up, flawed, not-good-enough people are, quite frankly, all that he has to choose from. There are very few Hollywood endings to be found; on the contrary, there is only story upon story of people who failed, yet God somehow used them anyway.

Don't believe me? Look at King David, the hand-selected man

after God's own heart, who managed to kill the giant Goliath with just a single stone but who also committed adultery, got his mistress pregnant, and then arranged for her husband to be killed in battle so no one would know what he did. Or Peter, who after three years of having a front-row seat to every miracle, and just hours after telling Jesus he would follow him to death, denied even *knowing* him, not once, but three times in a row. Even Paul, whose conversion on the road to Damascus was so powerful and dramatic that one might think he would never go astray, struggled with his own imperfection, lamenting that "good itself does not dwell in me, that is, in my sinful nature. For I have the desire to do what is good, but I cannot carry it out. For I do not do the good I want to do, but the evil I do not want to do—this I keep on doing" (Romans 7:18–19).

We live in a do-it-yourself world, one that tells us again and again that if we can just try a little harder, do a little more, be a little better, we might just save ourselves. It is the same mentality that compels us to fill up our homes with stuff in the first place, because that stuff becomes the status symbol for the life we think we want. It is the same mentality that drives us to fill up our schedules, causing us to confuse busyness with meaning. We've stuffed ourselves to overflowing with the pressure to achieve.

But it doesn't have to be that way.

In the End, There's Only Grace

I'm not proud of the messes I've made—or the ones I continue to make—and I don't relish the thought of airing my dirty laundry and sordid past for everyone else to see. I'd so much rather be writing this book as one who made all the right choices along the way, who runs my home with clocklike precision and efficiency and who is now ready to share my profound wisdom with the world. One who is, in every possible way, the very definition of what it means to be unstuffed.

Clearly I'm not that girl.

I am a work in progress, still flawed, still messing up daily. But I think that's the point. We're all a work in progress.

And we're all in need of grace.

Learning how to stop the incoming flow of stuff in our lives; learning how to ruthlessly purge, set limits, and value quality over quantity; learning how to find balance in the midst of a hectic schedule; discovering solutions for our paper problem and resolution to the guilt we feel over other people's stuff; learning to value real relationships in our life; taking the time to rest—all of those things are valuable lessons worth learning and refining and striving for.

But in the end, if we are trying to do all these things simply to save ourselves, we are doomed to fail. In *Counterfeit Gods*, New York City pastor Timothy Keller points out that nearly anything and everything can become an idol in our lives—something we prioritize, love, trust, and even obey in place of God.[27] It strikes me that the very process of decluttering our lives might cause us to uncover the things we have been valuing above all else—things like a nice home, our kids, a busy schedule, a successful career, an elevated social status, or even things that are less tangible, like feeling good about ourselves or simply just wanting to be happy.

But with all these pursuits, despite how important and valuable they might appear to be, we will inevitably find that something is still missing. After all, what happens when happiness fails us? Or when our social status crumbles? Or when our kids let us down? Or when our job is downsized? We may declutter our homes, unstuff our schedules, and de-stress our lives, sweeping them clean, and putting them in order, but what then? Who—or what—will fill that space?

In the end, salvation starts and ends with grace.

The only way to become truly unstuffed is to accept the amazing, incredible, unlimited, and *totally undeserved* grace we've already been given and to stop trying to fill that hole ourselves. Grace is the answer we are often too stubborn to believe and too proud to receive.

Remember that birthday party disaster, the one that so overwhelmed me I just had to walk away? Well, there's a little bit more to that story. You see, shortly after I returned to the party, one of the other moms happened to notice that giant mess as well. While the rest of us were distracted by birthday cake, a piñata, and face painting, she snuck in and methodically cleaned up the whole room without saying a word. After all the guests had left, I finally worked up the courage to start cleaning, only to find it had already been done. To this day, I still don't know which of my sweet friends was the angel who cleaned up that room, but I will *never* forget that overwhelming feeling of relief and gratitude.

My friends, God's grace is *so* much bigger than that! God loves us, not because we are perfect, but because *he* is. He doesn't care for us because we have all the answers or because we've figured out how to live unstuffed lives; on the contrary, he wants us to live an unstuffed life because he cares for us so much. The gift has already been given. The work has already been done.

And I don't know about you, but I can't think of a better way to become unstuffed than to finally recognize, understand, and truly believe that my slate has been wiped clean, once and for all.

With so much love and gratitude . . .

. . . To my husband, Chuck, for supporting me and cheering me on no matter what, for encouraging me when I feel like quitting, for challenging me when I need to be pushed, for making me laugh, for your daily breakfast sandwiches, and for still loving me — despite my filling our home with way too much stuff, then getting rid of it all and writing a book about it. You are the sharpener of my sword and the keeper of my heart. I love you.

. . . To my daughters, Maggie and Annie, for opening my heart to a love I never knew was even possible. Thank you for being patient when Mommy has to work, for not minding all those mornings I had to go to work early, for your cuddles and sweetness and our silly times together. Thank you for Rock-a-Bye and "High, Low, & Interesting," for selfies and our mommy-daughter dates. I love you both, to the moon and back!

. . . To my own family and my husband's family, for cheering me on from afar, and for believing in me even when I didn't believe in myself. To my sister, Beth — thank you for always being there, for our sista-sista chats, and for talking me off the ledge more than once. Paul and Jackie — thank you for coming all the way to Florida to remind me what family is really about.

. . . To my dearest friends, both old and new, who prayed for me, cheered me on, and walked with me through this crazy, nerve-racking, self-doubting process of writing a book. Alysha, Edie, Heather, Melanie, Michele, Bonnie, Melissa, LeeAnn, Natalie, and Bree — your sweet friendship and words of encouragement when I needed them most have meant the world to me. To Kasey, without whom book writing would have never even happened. I can't ever thank any of you enough.

… To all the people on the Zondervan team—I know I can't name every single one of you, but know that I am so grateful and honored to have the opportunity to work with such an incredible, God-fearing group of people. Carolyn: I adore you. Thank you for seeing something in that pile of manuscripts and for picking me. Thank you for your friendship and your encouragement. Lori: I am so grateful to be able to work with you. Thank you for pulling the best out of me, for your patience, your kindness, your willingness to push back when I need it, and for believing in me even when all seemed lost. Dirk: Thank you for your insight, your patience, and your kind and gentle spirit. Alicia: Thank you for your vision, for your get-it-done attitude, for believing in this project, and for all of your amazing hard work. Curt: Thank you for seeing our vision and creating the perfect package. People do judge a book by its cover! Jennifer: Thank you for your enthusiasm and support!

… To my literary agent, Andrew Wolgemuth, for stepping up and stepping in, even when you didn't have to. Words cannot express how grateful I am for your support, assistance, and graciousness.

… And last, but definitely not least, to my own amazing, incredible, hardworking, and just plain AWESOME team. You ladies rock, day in and day out, and I could not do any of this without you. Thank you for believing in the LWSL mission, for your positive attitudes and incredible talent, and for the love, laughter, and sense of purpose that happen in our office every single day.

Notes

1. From a lecture titled "The Beauty of Life," quoted in Norman Kelvin, ed., *William Morris on Art and Socialism* (Mineola, NY: Dover, 1999), 53.

2. Charles Duhigg, *The Power of Habit* (New York: Random House, 2012).

3. Ibid., chapter 7.

4. Lysa TerKeurst, "It's Almost Here ... *The Best Yes*," July 5, 2014, http://lysaterkeurst.com/2014/07/its-almost-here-the-best-yes/ (accessed September 13, 2015).

5. Sarah Sloat, "From the Expat Blog: Germany's Quiet Sundays," *Wall Street Journal*, March 23, 2015, www.wsj.com/articles/from-the-wsj-expat-blog-germanys-quiet-sundays-1427151283 (accessed July 15, 2015).

6. Glynnis Whitwer, *Taming the To-Do List* (Grand Rapids: Revell, 2015), 42.

7. SINTEF, "Big Data, for better or worse: 90% of world's data generated over last two years," *Science Daily*, www.sciencedaily.com/releases/2013/05/130522085217.htm (accessed July 15, 2015).

8. Eric Schmidt, "Every 2 Days We Create As Much Information As We Did Up To 2003," August 4, 2010, *TechCrunch.com*, http://techcrunch.com/2010/08/04/schmidt-data/ (accessed July 15, 2015).

9. See Guy Winch, "10 Things You Didn't Know about Guilt," *Psychology Today*, November 9, 2014, www.psychologytoday.com/blog/the-squeaky-wheel/201411/10-things-you-didnt-know-about-guilt (accessed July 15, 2015).

10. Quoted in Elizabeth Fenner, "The Top Six Excuses for Clutter," *Real Simple*, www.realsimple.com/home-organizing/organizing/top-causes-clutter (accessed July 15, 2015).

11. Kathy Waddill, *The Organizing Sourcebook* (New York: McGraw Hill, 2001), 192.

12. See Marie Kondo, *The Life-Changing Magic of Tidying Up* (New York: Ten Speed Press, 2014).

13. Eleanor Roosevelt, *You Learn by Living* (Louisville: Westminster John Knox, 1960), 29–30.

14. See Sherrie Bourg Carter, "The Hidden Health Hazards of Toxic Relationships," *Psychology Today*, August 2011, www.psychology today.com/blog/high-octane-women/201108/the-hidden-health -hazards-toxic-relationships (accessed July 15, 2015).

15. Carissa Andrews, "How Toxic Relationships Affect Your Health," *Canadian Pharmacy King*, November 24, 2014, www.canadian pharmacyking.com/KingsBlog/index.php/2014/11/How-Toxic -Relationships-Affect-Your-Health/ (accessed July 15, 2015).

16. University of Arizona, "Superficial Relationships Lead to Feelings of Detachment, Health-Related Problems," *News-medical .net*, June 23, 2010, www.news-medical.net/news/20100623/Superficial -relationships-lead-to-feelings-of-detachment-health-related-problems .aspx (accessed July 15, 2015).

17. Joseph Goldberg, "The Effects of Stress on Your Body," *WebMD*, June 24, 2014, www.webmd.com/balance/stress-manage ment/effects-of-stress-on-your-body (accessed July 15, 2015).

18. Better Sleep Council, "Sleep Statistics & Research: Americans Know How to Get Better Sleep—But Don't Act on It," *BetterSleep .org*, http://bettersleep.org/better-sleep/the-science-of-sleep/sleep -statistics-research/better-sleep-survey (accessed July 15, 2015).

19. Jeffrey M. Jones, "In U.S., 40% Get Less Than Recommended Amount of Sleep," *Gallup.com*, December 19, 2013, www.gallup.com/poll/166553/less-recommended-amount-sleep.aspx (accessed July 15, 2015).

20. Jeanie Lerche Davis, "The Toll of Sleep Loss in America," *WebMD*, November 29, 2011, www.webmd.com/sleep-disorders/features/toll-of-sleep-loss-in-america (accessed July 15, 2015).

21. Christopher Drake et al., "Caffeine Effects on Sleep Taken 0, 3, or 6 Hours before Going to Bed," *Journal of Clinical Sleep Medicine* 9, no. 11: 1195–1200, www.aasmnet.org/jcsm/acceptedpapers/jc-083-13.pdf (accessed July 15, 2015).

22. James Vlahos, "Is Sitting a Lethal Activity," *New York Times Magazine* April 14, 2011, www.nytimes.com/2011/04/17/magazine/mag-17sitting-t.html (accessed July 15, 2015).

23. "Your Office Chair Is Killing You," *BloombergBusiness online*, April 29, 2010, www.bloomberg.com/bw/magazine/content/10_19/b4177071221162.htm (accessed July 15, 2015).

24. Tony Schwartz, "Relax! You'll Be More Productive," *New York Times*, February 9, 2013, www.nytimes.com/2013/02/10/opinion/sunday/relax-youll-be-more-productive.html (accessed July 15, 2015).

25. Peter Haas, "The Jaw Dropping Benefits of Church Attendance," *PeterHaas.org*, August 19, 2014, www.peterhaas.org/?p=1342 (accessed July 15, 2015).

26. See, for example, Stephanie Watson, "Volunteering May Be Good for Body and Mind," *Harvard Health Blog*, June 26, 2013, www.health.harvard.edu/blog/volunteering-may-be-good-for-body-and-mind-201306266428 (accessed August 4, 2015).

27. Timothy Keller, *Counterfeit Gods* (New York: Dutton, 2009), xv–xviii.

Resources

To get more information on the resources mentioned in several places in the book and to access the free, printable resources, please visit Unstuffed.com/resources.

GET *unstuffed* ON THE GO

The new Unstuffed app will inspire and empower you to finally declutter, not just your home, but your mind and soul as well. Delivering daily decluttering challenges that combine social support, creative solutions, photo inspiration, and small actions to help you take back your life from all of the stuff that is weighing you down!

App Store

Google play

www.UnstuffedApp.com

Unstuffed

A DVD Study

Ruth Soukup

Have you ever wished you could get rid of all the STUFF weighing you down, once and for all? Do you long to find balance and order? Are you unsure of where to even start?

Ruth Soukup, *New York Times* bestselling author and popular blogger, knows all too well how overwhelming it can feel to have a life filled with too many things. Join Ruth in this four-session video study as she uses personal stories, biblical truth, and practical action plans to inspire and empower you to finally declutter not only your home but your mind and soul as well.

This DVD also includes a free introduction video as well as a printable study guide for groups and individuals.

Available in stores and online!

Living Well, Spending Less

12 Secrets of the Good Life

Ruth Soukup

Have you ever felt like your life—and budget—is spiraling out of control? Do you sometimes wish you could pull yourself together but wonder exactly how to manage all the scattered pieces of a chaotic life? Is it possible to find balance?

In a word, yes.

Ruth Soukup knows firsthand how stressful an unorganized life and budget can be. Through personal stories, biblical truth, and practical action plans, she will inspire you to make real and lasting changes to your personal goals, home, and finances in order to create the life you've always wanted—the Good Life. With brutal honesty and the wisdom of someone who has been there, Ruth will help you:

- Overcome the destructive cycle of "more is never enough" by learning to choose contentment.
- Step off the treadmill of trying to keep up and instead take back your time by making simple shifts in your daily habits.
- Stop busting your budget and learn to cut your grocery bill in half by making five simple tweaks to the way you shop.
- Bring order to a messy life and create a practical cleaning schedule that works for your own home and family.
- Develop a concrete plan for sharing the Good Life with others in order to bring lasting joy.

Available in stores and online!